SPICE IT UP!

Spices have a mystique all of their own. Associated with the exotic, wars have been fought over them, men have died in their quest and in times past spices have been used in place of gold and money. While today they may be considered inexpensive and an everyday commodity there is no denying that a pinch of chilli, a grind of pepper or a teaspoon of ginger will add that special touch to a dish. This book packed with recipes and information on spices presents you with dishes to suit any occasion.

CONTENTS

THE PANTRY SHELF

Unless otherwise stated, the following ingredients used in this book are:

Cream — Double, suitable for whipping

Flour — White flour, plain or standard

Sugar — White sugar

WHAT'S IN A TABLESPOON?

NEW ZEALAND
1 tablespoon =
15 mL OR 3 teaspoons

UNITED KINGDOM
1 tablespoon =
15 mL OR 3 teaspoons

AUSTRALIA
1 tablespoon =
20 mL OR 4 teaspoons

The recipes in this book were tested in Australia where a 20 mL tablespoon is standard. All measures are level.

The tablespoon in the New Zealand and United Kingdom sets of measuring spoons is 15 mL. In many recipes this difference will not matter. For recipes using baking powder, gelatine, bicarbonate of soda, small quantities of flour and cornflour, simply add another teaspoon for each tablespoon specified.

STARTERS

*These spicy, full-flavoured starters are sure to be popular.
Creamy guacamole served with tortillas is the perfect first course
for a casual dinner, while the hearty pumpkin soup flavoured
with cumin and nutmeg makes a great start to a winter meal.*

Hot Chilli Prawns

HOT CHILLI PRAWNS

1.5 kg/3 lb uncooked large prawns,
shelled and deveined, tails left intact

CHILLI MARINADE
2 teaspoons cracked black peppercorns
2 tablespoons chilli sauce
1 tablespoon soy sauce
1 clove garlic, crushed
1/4 cup/60 mL/2 fl oz lemon juice

MANGO CREAM
1 mango, roughly chopped
3 tablespoons coconut milk

1   To make marinade, place black
peppercorns, chilli sauce, soy sauce, garlic
and lemon juice in a bowl and mix to
combine. Add prawns, toss to coat, cover
and set aside to marinate for 1 hour. Toss
several times during marinating.

2   To make Mango Cream, place mango
flesh and coconut milk in a food processor
or blender and process until smooth.

3   Drain prawns and stir-fry in a lightly
oiled preheated frying pan or on a lightly
oiled barbecue for 3-4 minutes or until
prawns just change colour.

Serves 6

Coconut milk can be
purchased in a number of
forms: canned, or as a long-
life product in cartons, or as
a powder to which you add
water. Once it is opened it
has a short life and should be
used within a day or so. It is
available from Asian food
stores and some
supermarkets.

CURRIED ONION PUFFS

24 prepared small choux puff cases or
small cooked vol-au-vent pastry cases

CURRIED ONION FILLING
30 g/1 oz butter
2 onions, chopped
2 teaspoons flour
2 teaspoons curry powder
1/2 cup/125 mL/4 fl oz cream (double)
freshly ground black pepper

1   To make filling, melt butter in a
saucepan over a medium heat, add onions
and cook, stirring, for 5 minutes or until
onions are golden brown and soft. Stir in
flour and curry powder and cook for 1
minute longer.

2   Stir in cream, bring to the boil and
cook, stirring constantly, until mixture
boils and thickens. Season to taste with
black pepper.

3   Spoon filling into choux puffs or vol-
au-vent cases, place puffs on oven trays
and bake for 10 minutes or until heated
through.

Makes 24

Oven temperature
180°C, 350°F, Gas 4

Curry powder is a
combination of spices which
usually includes turmeric,
coriander, chilli, cumin,
ginger, black pepper,
fenugreek and cardamom.

CURRIED SALMON ROLLS

Oven temperature
180°C, 350°F, Gas 4

440 g/14 oz canned salmon, drained,
bones and skin removed, flesh flaked
125 g/4 oz grated tasty cheese
(mature Cheddar)
3 gherkins, chopped
2 tablespoons mayonnaise
1 tablespoon fruit chutney
4 spring onions, chopped
2 teaspoons curry powder
freshly ground black pepper
1 loaf sliced white bread
60 g/2 oz butter, melted

1   Place salmon, cheese, gherkins,
mayonnaise, chutney, spring onions,
curry powder and black pepper to taste in
a bowl and mix to combine.

2   Trim crusts from twenty bread slices
and, using a rolling pin, slightly flatten
each slice. Spread each slice of bread with
salmon mixture, roll up and secure with a
toothpick.

3   Place rolls on a lightly greased baking
tray, brush with melted butter and bake
for 15 minutes or until golden and heated
through.

Makes 20

These rolls are also delicious
made with canned tuna or
cooked chicken in place of
the salmon.

Left: *Curried Salmon Rolls*
Below: *Pumpkin and Apple Soup*

PUMPKIN AND APPLE SOUP

30 g/1 oz butter
2 onions, chopped
2 cloves garlic, crushed
1 teaspoon ground cumin
$^{1}/_{2}$ teaspoon ground nutmeg
2 stalks celery, chopped
1 kg/2 lb pumpkin, chopped
2 green apples, peeled, cored
and chopped
6 cups/1.5 litres/2$^{1}/_{2}$ pt chicken stock
freshly ground black pepper

1   Melt butter in a large saucepan, add onions and garlic and cook over a medium heat, stirring constantly, for 5 minutes or until onions are soft. Stir in cumin and nutmeg and cook for 1 minute longer.

2   Add celery, pumpkin, apples and stock and bring to the boil. Reduce heat, cover and simmer for 25-30 minutes or until vegetables are tender.

3   Transfer soup to a food processor or blender and process until smooth. Return to a clean saucepan, bring to simmering, season to taste with black pepper and serve.

Serves 4

This hearty soup can stand alone for a great winter's lunch dish, or serve it with crusty bread and follow with a cheese and fruit platter for a complete meal.

GUACAMOLE WITH TORTILLAS

Oven temperature
180°C, 350°F, Gas 4

Guacamole is also delicious served as a dip with a selection of raw and lightly cooked vegetables. Raw vegetables could include carrot and celery sticks, tiny radishes, red, green and yellow pepper strips; lightly cooked vegetables might include cauliflower and broccoli florets, asparagus spears and snow peas (mangetout).

6 corn tortillas

CHILLI BUTTER
90 g/3 oz butter
2 teaspoons finely grated lemon rind
2 teaspoons chilli sauce
1 teaspoon ground cumin

GUACAMOLE
1 avocado, halved, stoned and peeled
1 tomato, peeled and finely chopped
2 tablespoons lemon juice
1 tablespoon finely chopped fresh coriander or parsley

1   To make Chilli Butter, place butter, lemon rind, chilli sauce and cumin in a bowl and mix to combine.

2   To make Guacamole, place avocado in a bowl and mash with a fork. Stir in tomato, lemon juice and coriander or parsley.

3   Place tortillas in a single layer on a baking tray and heat in oven for 3-5 minutes or until warm. To serve, place Chilli Butter, Guacamole and tortillas on a platter so that each person can spread a tortilla with Chilli Butter, top with Guacamole, then roll up and eat.

Serves 6

CHEESE AND BACON NACHOS

Oven temperature
180°C, 350°F, Gas 4

Jalapeño chillies are medium green to dark green chillies that taper to a blunt end and are 5-7.5 cm/2-3 in long and 2-2.5 cm/³/₄-1 in wide. They are medium-to-hot in taste and are also available canned or bottled.

6 rashers bacon, finely chopped
6 spring onions, finely chopped
4 jalapeño chillies, finely chopped
200 g/6¹/₂ oz packet corn chips
125 g/4 oz grated tasty cheese
(mature Cheddar)
1 cup/250 g/8 oz sour cream

1   Cook bacon, spring onions and chillies in a nonstick frying pan over a medium heat for 4-5 minutes or until bacon is crisp. Remove from pan and drain on absorbent kitchen paper.

2   Place corn chips in a shallow ovenproof dish and sprinkle with bacon mixture and cheese. Bake for 5-8 minutes or until heated through and cheese is melted. Serve immediately, accompanied with sour cream for dipping.

Serves 6

Guacamole with Tortillas,
Cheese and Bacon Nachos

MUSHROOMS WITH CHILLI BUTTER

20 button mushrooms, stalks removed

CHILLI BUTTER
60 g/2 oz butter
$^1/_2$ fresh red chilli, finely chopped
$^1/_2$ teaspoon ground cumin
**1 tablespoon finely chopped
fresh parsley**

1   To make Chilli Butter, place butter, chilli, cumin and parsley in a food processor or blender and process until smooth. Shape butter into a log, wrap in plastic food wrap and chill until required.

2   Cut butter log into twenty pieces, place one piece on each mushroom and cook under a preheated grill for 4-5 minutes or until butter melts and mushrooms are cooked. Serve immediately with toothpicks so that your guests can spear a mushroom then eat it.

Makes 20

When handling fresh chillies do not put your hands near your eyes or allow them to touch your lips. To avoid discomfort and burning, wear rubber gloves. Freshly minced chilli is also available in jars from supermarkets.

DEVILLED MIXED NUTS

45 g/1¹/₂ oz butter
2 cloves garlic, crushed
1 teaspoon Worcestershire sauce
2 teaspoons curry powder
pinch cayenne pepper
125 g/4 oz blanched almonds
125 g/4 oz cashew nuts
125 g/4 oz pecan nuts or walnuts

1   Melt butter in a small saucepan, stir in garlic, Worcestershire sauce, curry powder and cayenne.

2   Place almonds, cashew nuts and pecans or walnuts in an ovenproof dish. Pour over butter mixture and toss to coat nuts.

3   Bake nuts, stirring every 5 minutes, for 15-20 minutes or until they are toasted. Allow nuts to cool, then store in an airtight container.

Serves 6

Oven temperature
180°C, 350°F, Gas 4

For a special occasion you might like to decorate a bowl of devilled nuts with a chilli flower.
To make a chilli flower, choose a small chilli or trim the ends from a long chilli, keeping the stem end intact. Using a small pair of scissors cut around the chilli to form petals, taking care not to cut all the way to the stem. Remove the seeds, drop the chilli into a bowl of iced water and refrigerate until the 'flower' opens out.

MAIN MEALS

In this chapter you will find interesting main meals that rely on spices to tempt the taste buds. There are curries, of course, but don't forget to try some of the other recipes, such as Spiced Calamari or Hot Chilli Pork Spareribs, the next time you are looking for a little something to spice up your life.

Hot Chicken Curry

Steak with Mustard Sauce

Cajun Burgers

Dry Beef Curry

Curried Chicken Kebabs

Seafood Kebabs

Frankfurter Casserole

Chilli Con Carne

Pork Vindaloo

Beef and Tomato Curry

Hot Chilli Pork Spareribs

Spicy Vegetables

Skewered Pork

Spiced Calamari

Hot Chicken Curry

HOT CHICKEN CURRY

10 baby new potatoes, scrubbed
and halved
2 onions, cut into eighths
1 clove garlic, crushed
$^1/_2$ teaspoon hot curry paste (Vindaloo)
440 g/14 oz canned tomatoes,
undrained and mashed
1 cup/250 mL/8 fl oz chicken stock
2 tablespoons dry white wine
2 tablespoons mango chutney
3 teaspoons curry powder
2 teaspoons ground cumin
4 tablespoons tomato purée
2 chicken breast fillets, cut into
2 cm/$^3/_4$ in cubes
1 tablespoon finely chopped
fresh coriander

1   Boil, steam or microwave potatoes until just tender. Set aside to cool.

2   Place onions, garlic, curry paste (Vindaloo) and 1 tablespoon juice from tomatoes in a saucepan and cook for 2-3 minutes or until onion is soft.

3   Combine tomatoes, stock, wine, chutney, curry powder, cumin and tomato purée. Stir into onion mixture and cook over a medium heat, stirring, for 2-3 minutes. Add chicken and potatoes and cook over a low heat for 10-15 minutes or until chicken is tender. Just prior to serving, sprinkle with coriander.

Serves 4

This easy, low-fat one-dish curry is ideal for weight watchers but will be enjoyed by the whole family. Serve with a green vegetable, such as beans, and for those not worried about kilojoules (calories), add rice.

STEAK WITH MUSTARD SAUCE

30 g/1 oz butter
4 lean rib eye or fillet steaks

FRENCH MUSTARD SAUCE
2 spring onions, chopped
1 tablespoon wholegrain mustard
2 teaspoons Dijon mustard
$^1/_2$ cup/125 mL/4 fl oz dry white wine
3 tablespoons water
1 teaspoon honey
$^1/_4$ teaspoon dried thyme
2 tablespoons cream (double)
2 tablespoons grated tasty cheese
(mature Cheddar)

1   Melt butter in a large frying pan, add steaks and cook for 4-5 minutes each side or until cooked to your liking. Remove steaks from pan, set aside and keep warm.

2   To make sauce, add spring onions to pan and cook for 1 minute. Stir in wholegrain mustard, Dijon mustard, wine, water, honey and thyme and cook over a medium heat, stirring, for 3-4 minutes or until sauce reduces slightly.

3   Remove pan from heat and stir in cream and cheese. To serve, spoon sauce over steaks.

Serves 4

The French Dijon mustard is probably the most famous prepared mustard. For mustard to be called Dijon it must be made to a strict recipe that uses black mustard seed, salt and spices with verjuice (a vinegar made from tart fruit, such as grapes or apples), wine or vinegar. Mustards varying from this recipe must be labelled 'Dijon-style'.

CAJUN BURGERS

2 tablespoons cracked black peppercorns
2 teaspoons paprika
4 beef medallions or fillet steaks,
each 3 cm/1¼ in thick
1 tablespoon vegetable oil
4 tablespoons prepared pasta sauce or
tomato relish
4 bread rolls, split and toasted
4 large lettuce leaves

1   Combine black peppercorns and paprika. Coat beef medallions or fillet steaks with pepper mixture. Heat oil in a large frying pan until it begins to smoke, add medallions or fillet steaks and cook over a medium heat for 3-4 minutes each side or until cooked to your liking.

2   Place pasta sauce or tomato relish in a small saucepan and cook over a medium heat for 2-3 minutes or until heated through.

3   Top bottom half of each roll with a lettuce leaf, then a medallion or fillet steak, a spoonful of sauce or relish and top half of roll. Serve immediately.

Serves 4

Paprika, cayenne pepper and chilli powder are all affected by light and over time will turn from a brick red colour to a dull brown. It is best to buy them in small quantities and to keep them in airtight containers away from light.

DRY BEEF CURRY

BEEF CURRY
60 g/2 oz ghee or clarified butter
500 g/1 lb chuck steak, cubed
1 large onion, chopped
2 fresh red chillies, sliced
2 cloves garlic, crushed
1 teaspoon ground coriander
1 teaspoon saffron powder
1 teaspoon ground cumin
1 teaspoon black mustard seeds
1 tablespoon ground garam masala
$^1/_2$ cup/125 mL/4 fl oz water
2 large tomatoes, peeled and chopped
2 curry leaves (optional)
1 small cinnamon stick
3 tablespoons natural yogurt

GOLDEN RICE
1 cup/220 g/7 oz long grain rice
2 cups/500 mL/16 fl oz coconut milk
$^1/_4$ teaspoon saffron powder
1 lime leaf (optional)
30 g/1 oz desiccated coconut

1   To make curry, melt 45 g/1$^1/_2$ oz ghee or butter in a large saucepan and cook meat in batches until brown on all sides. Remove meat from pan and set aside.

2   Melt remaining ghee or butter in pan, add onion and chillies and cook for 4-5 minutes or until onion is golden. Stir in garlic, coriander, saffron, cumin, mustard seeds and half the garam masala and cook for 1 minute longer.

3   Stir water, tomatoes, curry leaves and cinnamon stick into pan and bring to the boil. Reduce heat to simmering, return meat to pan, cover and simmer for 1$^1/_2$ hours or until meat is tender.

4   Remove pan from heat, stir in remaining garam masala and yogurt. Return pan to heat and simmer for 5 minutes. Remove cinnamon stick.

5   For the Golden Rice, place rice, coconut milk, saffron, lime leaf and coconut in a heavy-based saucepan. Bring to the boil, then reduce heat, cover and simmer for 20 minutes or until rice has absorbed the coconut milk and is tender.

Serves 4

Accompany curry with a selection of sambals. You might like to serve your curry with some of the following:
Banana Sambal: Combine 2 sliced bananas and 1 tablespoon lemon juice.
Coconut Sambal: Combine $^3/_4$ cup/60 g/2 oz desiccated coconut, 1 tablespoon finely chopped onion, 1 small fresh red chilli, seeded and chopped and 1 tablespoon lime juice.
Cucumber Sambal: Peel, seed and thinly slice 1 small cucumber and mix with $^1/_2$ cup/125 g/4 oz natural yogurt.
Tomato Sambal: Chop 2 tomatoes and combine with 1 seeded and sliced fresh green chilli, 1 tablespoon lemon juice, 1 tablespoon finely chopped onion and 1 tablespoon desiccated coconut.

'The secret of a good curry depends on the initial cooking of the onions. Heat the ghee, clarified butter or oil first, add the onions and cook over a medium heat until golden. Stir gently throughout the cooking to avoid burning.'

CURRIED CHICKEN KEBABS

750 g/1¹/₂ lb chicken breast fillets, skin
removed, cut into 2.5 cm/1 in cubes

LIME CURRY GLAZE
1 cup/315 g/10 oz lime marmalade
2 tablespoons Dijon mustard
2 teaspoons curry powder
1 tablespoon lime juice

For a complete meal serve
kebabs, a mixed lettuce
salad and garlic baked
potatoes.
To make potatoes, scrub the
required number of large
potatoes and, using an
apple corer, carefully
remove a plug from each
potato, making sure not to
go right through the potato.
Reserve the plugs. For each
potato you will require 1
clove garlic, halved.
Combine 2 tablespoons olive
oil, 1 tablespoon finely
chopped fresh rosemary and
freshly ground black pepper
to taste. Fill hole in each
potato with two garlic halves
and a little oil mixture. Cut off
two-thirds of the plug and
discard. Replace remaining
plug in potato and wrap
potatoes in aluminium foil.
Cook potatoes on a
preheated barbecue or in
the oven at 180°C/350°F/
Gas 4 for 1 hour or until
tender.

1 To make glaze, place marmalade,
mustard, curry powder and lime juice in a
small saucepan and cook over a medium
heat, stirring, for 3 minutes or until
ingredients are combined. Remove from
heat and set aside to cool.

2 Thread chicken cubes onto twelve
oiled skewers. Place skewers in a shallow
glass or ceramic dish, spoon glaze over,
cover and set aside to marinate for at least
an hour.

3 Remove chicken from glaze and
reserve any remaining glaze. Cook kebabs
on a lightly oiled, preheated barbecue,
turning frequently and brushing with
reserved marinade for 8-10 minutes or
until cooked.

Makes 12

SEAFOOD KEBABS

8 mussels, removed from shells
1 large white fish fillet, cut into
8 x 2 cm/³/₄ in cubes
8 large uncooked prawns, shelled and
deveined, tails left intact
8 scallops
1 salmon fillet, cut into
8 x 2 cm/³/₄ in cubes

CHILLI LIME GLAZE
¹/₄ cup/60 mL/2 fl oz olive oil
2 fresh red chillies, seeded and
finely chopped
1 clove garlic, crushed
¹/₄ cup/60 mL/2 fl oz lime juice

1 Thread a mussel, a piece of white fish,
a prawn, a scallop and a piece of salmon
on to an oiled skewer. Repeat with
remaining seafood to make eight skewers.

2 To make glaze, place oil, chillies,
garlic and lime juice in a small bowl and
mix to combine.

3 Brush kebabs with glaze and cook on a
lightly oiled, preheated barbecue, turning
frequently and brushing with remaining
glaze, for 4-5 minutes or until seafood
changes colour and is cooked through.
Serve immediately.

Kebabs can be cooked
under a preheated grill rather
than on the barbecue if you
wish.

Makes 8

Seafood Kebabs,
Curried Chicken Kebabs

FRANKFURTER CASSEROLE

1 cup/200 g/6$^{1}/_2$ oz barley
60 g/2 oz butter
1 onion, chopped
125 g/4 oz mushrooms, sliced
3 rashers bacon, chopped
3 cups/750 mL/1$^{1}/_4$ pt chicken stock
$^{3}/_4$ cup/185 mL/6 fl oz dry white wine
1 teaspoon ground cumin
$^{1}/_2$ teaspoon ground coriander
$^{1}/_2$ cup/125 mL/4 fl oz cream (double)
500 g/1 lb thin frankfurters, cut
into 2 cm/$^{3}/_4$ in lengths

1   Place barley in a large bowl, cover with water and set aside to soak for 2 hours. Drain well and set aside.

2   Melt butter in a large saucepan, add onion, mushrooms and bacon and cook, stirring constantly, for 3 minutes.

3   Add barley, stock, wine, cumin and coriander and bring to the boil. Reduce heat, cover and simmer for 30 minutes or until liquid has been absorbed. Stir in cream and frankfurters and cook for 10 minutes longer.

Serves 4

All parts of the coriander plant can be used. However it is important to know that fresh and ground coriander have completely different flavours. Fresh coriander is the leaf and is a herb, whereas ground coriander is a spice and is the ground seeds of the plant.

CHILLI CON CARNE

1 tablespoon vegetable oil
2 onions, chopped
2 cloves garlic, crushed
$^1/_2$ red pepper, chopped
500 g/1 lb lean beef mince
440 g/14 oz canned tomatoes,
drained and chopped
$^1/_2$ teaspoon chilli powder
1 teaspoon ground cumin
1 teaspoon ground coriander
2 tablespoons tomato paste (purée)
315 g/10 oz canned red kidney beans,
drained and rinsed
$^1/_2$ cup/125 mL/4 fl oz beef stock

CORN BREAD
1 cup/170 g/5$^1/_2$ oz corn meal (polenta)
$^3/_4$ cup/90 g/3 oz self-raising flour, sifted
$^1/_2$ teaspoon sugar
15 g/$^1/_2$ oz butter, melted
1 cup/250 mL/8 fl oz milk
1 egg

1   Heat oil in a large frying pan, add onions, garlic and red pepper and cook over a medium heat, stirring, for 4-5 minutes or until onions are soft.

2   Stir in mince and cook for 10 minutes. Add tomatoes, chilli powder, cumin, coriander, tomato paste (purée), beans and stock and bring to the boil. Reduce heat and simmer for 25 minutes.

3   To make Corn Bread, place corn meal (polenta), flour and sugar in a bowl and mix to combine. Place melted butter, milk and egg in bowl and whisk to combine. Stir milk mixture into corn meal (polenta) mixture and mix to combine.

4   Spoon Corn Bread into a greased 20 cm/8 in round cake tin and bake for 15-20 minutes or until bread is cooked and golden. Serve Corn Bread warm with Chilli Con Carne.

Serves 4

Oven temperature
180°C, 350°F, Gas 4

Chillies are native to Mexico and have been grown there for at least nine thousand years.
Although cayenne pepper and paprika are both chilli powders, the products labelled as chilli powder or seasoning are usually a mixture of ground chillies, herbs and other spices. A typical chilli powder or seasoning might contain chillies, cumin, garlic, salt and oregano. This accounts for the difference you find in the strength of chilli powders or seasonings.

PORK VINDALOO

750 g/1¹/₂ lb lean pork, diced
2 onions, chopped
3 cloves garlic, crushed
440 g/14 oz canned tomatoes, undrained
and chopped
2 teaspoons ground cumin
2 teaspoons mustard seeds
2 teaspoons ground cinnamon
1 teaspoon ground turmeric
1 teaspoon chilli paste (sambal oelek)
¹/₄ cup/60 mL/2 fl oz white vinegar
1 tablespoon brown sugar
3 tablespoons natural yogurt
2 tablespoons lime juice
freshly ground black pepper
2 cups/500 mL/16 fl oz chicken stock
2 tablespoons chopped fresh coriander

1   Place pork, onions, garlic, tomatoes, cumin, mustard seeds, cinnamon, turmeric, chilli paste (sambal oelek), vinegar, sugar, yogurt, lime juice and black pepper to taste in a glass or ceramic bowl and mix to combine. Cover and marinate in the refrigerator for at least 3 hours.

2   Transfer pork mixture to a large saucepan, stir in stock and bring to simmering. Cover and simmer, stirring occasionally, for 1 hour or until pork is tender. Just prior to serving, stir in coriander.

Serves 6

Turmeric has a peppery aroma and a bitter warm taste. It is an important ingredient in curry powder and gives the yellow colour to many dishes, including curries, relishes and pickles. It is also used to colour some of the milder mustards.

BEEF AND TOMATO CURRY

3 tablespoons oil
750 g/1¹/₂ lb chuck steak, cut
into wide strips
3 onions, chopped
3 cloves garlic, crushed
1 tablespoon curry powder
1 tablespoon cumin seeds
2 teaspoons ground coriander
2 tablespoons tomato paste (purée)
1 tablespoon sweet fruit chutney
440 g/14 oz canned tomatoes,
undrained and mashed
1 cup/250 mL/8 fl oz beef stock

1   Heat oil in a large frying pan, add meat and cook over a high heat for 4-5 minutes or until meat is browned. Remove meat from pan and set aside.

2   Reduce heat to medium, add onions and garlic to pan and cook, stirring, for 4-5 minutes or until onions are soft. Add curry powder and cook for 1 minute longer. Return beef to the pan, then add cumin seeds, coriander, tomato paste (purée), chutney, tomatoes and stock and bring to the boil. Reduce heat, cover and simmer, stirring occasionally, for 1 hour or until meat is tender.

Serves 6

The best tasting spices are those that are freshly ground. A pestle and mortar is ideal for crushing small amounts of spice, while large quantities can be ground in a coffee grinder – kept for this purpose. Do not grind spices in the same grinder as you use for coffee, as the flavours mix and the result is spiced coffee or coffee-flavoured spices!

Hot Chilli Pork Spareribs

6 small pork back rib racks
freshly ground black pepper
$^1/_2$ cup/125 mL/4 fl oz apple juice
$^1/_4$ cup/60 mL/2 fl oz lime juice
dash Tabasco sauce

APPLE CHILLI GLAZE
1 tablespoon vegetable oil
2 onions, finely chopped
2 cloves garlic, crushed
1 fresh red chilli, seeded and chopped
125 g/4 oz canned apple purée
1 cup/315 g/10 oz apple jelly
$^1/_2$ cup/125 mL/4 fl oz apple juice
2 tablespoons lime juice

1   Season ribs with black pepper to taste and place in a shallow glass or ceramic dish. Combine apple juice, lime juice and Tabasco sauce, pour over ribs and toss to coat. Cover and refrigerate for 1-2 hours.

2   To make glaze, heat oil in a saucepan, add onions, garlic and chilli and cook over a medium heat for 10 minutes or until onions are soft. Stir in apple purée, jelly and juice, bring to simmering and simmer, stirring frequently, for 15 minutes or until mixture thickens. Stir in lime juice, season to taste with black pepper and simmer for 15 minutes longer.

3   Drain ribs, and reserve any remaining marinade. Sear ribs on a preheated lightly oiled barbecue for 5 minutes each side, frequently brushing with reserved marinade. Brush ribs with warm glaze and cook, turning, for 5 minutes longer. Serve ribs with remaining glaze.

Serves 6

You can cook these ribs under a preheated grill rather than on a barbecue if you wish. You will find that the cooking time is about the same and the result just as delicious.

Spicy Vegetables

3 tablespoons vegetable oil
1 large onion, sliced
4 cloves garlic, crushed
1 small fresh red chilli, seeded and finely chopped
1 teaspoon ground coriander
1 teaspoon black mustard seeds
2 large eggplant (aubergines), cut into 2.5 cm/1 in cubes
440 g/14 oz canned tomatoes, undrained and mashed
$^1/_2$ cup/125 mL/4 fl oz chicken stock
2.5 cm/1 in piece of cinnamon stick
freshly ground black pepper

1   Heat oil in a large saucepan, add onion and cook for 5 minutes or until golden. Add garlic, chilli, coriander and mustard seeds and cook for 1 minute longer.

2   Add eggplant (aubergines) and stir-fry for 1-2 minutes. Stir in tomatoes, stock and cinnamon stick and bring to the boil. Reduce heat and simmer for 25-30 minutes or until eggplant (aubergines) are tender and mixture thickens. Remove cinnamon stick and season vegetables to taste with black pepper.

Serves 4

Serve this wonderful fusion of eggplant (aubergines), tomatoes and spices with brown rice and plenty of natural yogurt.

Hot Chilli Pork Spareribs

SKEWERED PORK

750 g/1 1/2 lb pork fillets, sliced

GINGER MARINADE
1 teaspoon grated fresh ginger
1 onion, chopped
1/2 cup/125 mL/4 fl oz soy sauce
3 tablespoons brown sugar
1/3 cup/90 mL/3 fl oz dry sherry

1 To make marinade, place ginger, onion, soy sauce, brown sugar and sherry in a glass or ceramic bowl. Add pork and toss well to coat. Cover and refrigerate for 2 hours.

2 Remove pork from marinade and thread onto eight oiled skewers. Cook skewers on a preheated lightly oiled barbecue or under a preheated grill, basting frequently with marinade, for 6-8 minutes or until cooked.

Makes 8

This marinated pork has an exquisite flavour and is especially good when cooked on the barbecue.

SPICED CALAMARI

500 g/1 lb calamari (squid) rings
vegetable oil for deep-frying

SPICY MARINADE
2 teaspoons tamarind paste or
tomato paste (purée)
1/4 teaspoon ground saffron
1 teaspoon grated fresh ginger
2 cloves garlic, crushed
1 tablespoon teriyaki sauce
1/3 cup/90 mL/3 fl oz vegetable oil

BATTER
1 1/4 cups/155 g/5 oz flour
1/3 cup/90 mL/3 fl oz water
1 egg, beaten
freshly ground black pepper

1 To make marinade, place tamarind paste, saffron, ginger, garlic, teriyaki sauce and oil in a glass or ceramic bowl and mix to combine. Add calamari (squid) rings and toss to coat. Cover and refrigerate for at least 1 hour.

2 To make batter, place flour in a mixing bowl and gradually stir in water, then egg until smooth. Season to taste with black pepper. Set aside.

3 Heat oil in a large saucepan until a cube of bread dropped in browns in 50 seconds. Drain calamari (squid), dip in batter and cook a few at a time in hot oil until golden and crisp. Drain on absorbent kitchen paper and serve immediately.

Serves 4

The secret to this dish is the marinade. The longer you can leave the calamari (squid) to marinate the better the flavour will be.

*Spiced Calamari, Spicy Vegetables,
Skewered Pork*

VEGETARIAN

Here is a collection of delicious meat-free main course dishes which make the most of vegetable and spice combinations. Next time you are looking for a spicy main meal why not try Potato Curry in Filo Cups or Vegetarian Chilli?

Indonesian Salad

INDONESIAN SALAD

¹/₄ cabbage, shredded
250 g/8 oz green beans, sliced
1 carrot, cut into matchsticks
8 baby new potatoes, scrubbed
and halved
1 cucumber, cut into matchsticks
4 hard-boiled eggs, quartered

SATAY DRESSING
1 tablespoon vegetable oil
1 onion, chopped
1 clove garlic, crushed
1 teaspoon ground cumin
1 teaspoon curry powder
¹/₂ teaspoon ground coriander
1 tablespoon white vinegar
1 tablespoon brown sugar
¹/₂ cup/125 g/4 oz crunchy
peanut butter
2 tablespoons fruit chutney
1¹/₂ cups/375 mL/12 fl oz water

1   Boil, steam or microwave cabbage, beans, carrot and potatoes, separately, until just tender. Chill.

2   To make dressing, heat oil in a saucepan, add onion and garlic and cook for 2 minutes. Stir in cumin, curry powder and coriander and cook for 1 minute longer. Add vinegar, sugar, peanut butter, chutney and water, bring to simmering and simmer, stirring occasionally, for 15 minutes or until dressing thickens. Remove pan from heat and set aside to cool to room temperature. To serve, arrange cooked vegetables, cucumber, eggs and dressing attractively on a large serving platter.

Serves 4 as a main meal

This version of the popular Indonesian salad *gado-gado* makes a great main meal for vegetarians or can be an interesting school or office lunch. For a packed lunch simply place the dressing in a small container with a well-fitting lid and arrange the vegetables and eggs attractively in a lunch box.

VEGETABLES IN GINGER SAUCE

60 g/2 oz butter
2 onions, cut into eighths
1 clove garlic, crushed
2 teaspoons grated fresh ginger
1 teaspoon ground coriander
1 large parsnip, cubed
2 large turnips, cubed
1 large carrot, sliced
1 sweet potato, cut into chunks
6 baby new potatoes, scrubbed
1¹/₂ cups/375 mL/12 fl oz orange juice
1 cup/250 mL/8 fl oz vegetable stock
1 tablespoon cornflour blended with
¹/₄ cup/60 mL/2 fl oz water
freshly ground black pepper
1 leek, chopped
2 tablespoons snipped fresh chives
1 tablespoon finely grated orange rind

1   Melt butter in a large saucepan, add onion and garlic and cook for 3-4 minutes or until onion is soft. Stir in ginger and coriander and cook for 1 minute longer. Add parsnip, turnips, carrot, sweet potato, potatoes, orange juice and stock. Cover and bring to the boil. Reduce heat and simmer for 25 minutes or until vegetables are tender. Remove vegetables, using a slotted spoon, and set aside.

2   Stir cornflour mixture into liquid and season to taste with black pepper. Bring liquid to the boil and boil, stirring constantly, for 5 minutes, or until sauce thickens. Return vegetables to pan, add leek, chives and orange rind and cook for 5 minutes longer or until heated through.

Serves 4

To store fresh ginger, peel and place in a glass jar. Cover with sherry or green ginger wine, store in the refrigerator and use as you would fresh ginger. Ginger will keep in this way for many months. The sherry or wine left after the ginger is used is ideal to use in cooking or dressings.

Right: Potato-filled Peppers
Far right: Vegetarian Chilli

POTATO-FILLED PEPPERS

Oven temperature
180°C, 350°F, Gas 4

The secret to this recipe is the garam masala. Garam masala is a highly scented mix of cardamom seeds, cinnamon stick, nutmeg, mace and cumin seeds. Sometimes cloves and coriander are added for extra zest. It can be found in the herb and spice section of any supermarket.

6 green or red peppers
60 g/2 oz butter
1 small fresh red chilli, seeded and chopped
1 onion, chopped
4 potatoes, cooked, peeled and cubed
$\frac{1}{2}$ teaspoon ground coriander
$\frac{1}{4}$ teaspoon ground cumin
$\frac{1}{2}$ teaspoon mustard seeds
$\frac{1}{2}$ teaspoon ground turmeric
$\frac{1}{2}$ teaspoon garam masala
2 teaspoons lemon juice

1   Cut a slice from the top of each pepper. Remove seeds, keeping shells intact. Drop peppers into a saucepan of boiling water and cook for 3 minutes. Drain, refresh under cold running water and pat dry with absorbent kitchen paper.

2   Melt butter in a large frying pan, add chilli, onion and potatoes and stir-fry over a medium heat for 5 minutes or until potatoes are golden brown. Stir in coriander, cumin, mustard seeds, turmeric and garam masala and cook, stirring, for 1-2 minutes longer. Sprinkle with lemon juice.

3   Spoon potato mixture into pepper shells, place shells in a lightly greased baking dish and bake for 20 minutes.

Serves 6

Vegetarian Chilli

2 tablespoons vegetable oil
2 onions, cut into eighths
3 cloves garlic, crushed
2 carrots, sliced
1 red pepper, chopped
1 green pepper, chopped
250 g/8 oz pumpkin, diced
2 teaspoons chilli paste (sambal oelek)
1 teaspoon dried oregano
2 teaspoons ground cumin
4 tomatoes, cut into eighths
3 tablespoons tomato paste (purée)
$^1/_2$ cup/125 mL/4 fl oz tomato sauce
2 tablespoons Worcestershire sauce
2 cups/500 mL/16 fl oz vegetable stock
or water
2 x 440 g/14 oz canned red kidney
beans, drained and rinsed
250 g/8 oz green beans, cut into
2.5 cm/1 in lengths
250 g/8 oz baby squash, quartered
4 zucchini (courgettes), sliced
freshly ground black pepper
2 avocados, halved, stoned and peeled
1 tablespoon lemon juice
1 cup/250 g/8 oz sour cream or
natural yogurt

1   Heat oil in a large saucepan, add onions and garlic and cook for 5 minutes or until onions are soft. Add carrots, red and green pepper and pumpkin and cook for 5 minutes longer.

2   Stir in chilli paste (sambal oelek), oregano, cumin, tomatoes, tomato paste (purée), tomato sauce, Worcestershire sauce, stock or water and red kidney beans and bring to the boil. Reduce heat, cover and simmer for 25 minutes or until vegetables are almost tender. Add green beans, squash and zucchini (courgettes) and cook for 10 minutes longer or until all vegetables are tender. Season to taste with black pepper.

3   Place avocados, lemon juice and black pepper to taste in a bowl and mash. Serve avocado mixture and sour cream or yogurt with Vegetarian Chilli.

Serves 6

All this delicious medley of vegetables needs to make a complete meal is crusty bread or wholemeal rolls. For something different you might like to serve it with warmed pitta bread rounds.

Tofu with Curry Sauce

3 tablespoons peanut (groundnut) oil
2 cloves garlic, crushed
1 tablespoon medium curry paste
1 tablespoon brown sugar
2 tablespoons soy sauce
$^1/4$ cup/60 mL/2 fl oz vegetable stock
$^1/2$ cup/125 mL/4 fl oz coconut milk
500 g/1 lb tofu, cut into
2 cm/$^3/4$ in cubes

1   Heat oil in a frying pan, add garlic and cook over a medium heat for 1 minute. Stir in curry paste, sugar, soy sauce, stock and coconut milk, bring to simmering and simmer for 5 minutes or until sauce reduces and thickens slightly.

2   Arrange tofu on a serving platter, spoon sauce over and serve immediately.

Serves 4

Curry pastes are available from most supermarkets and all Oriental and Asian food stores.

BARLEY AND VEGETABLE CURRY

60 g/2 oz butter
4 leeks, sliced
2 cloves garlic, crushed
2 teaspoons curry powder
$^1/_2$ teaspoon garam masala
1$^1/_2$ cups/300 g/9$^1/_2$ oz pearl barley
2 large potatoes, cut into
2 cm/$^3/_4$ in cubes
375 g/12 oz pumpkin, cut into
2 cm/$^3/_4$ in cubes
4 cups/1 litre/1$^3/_4$ pt vegetable stock
or water
250 g/8 oz broccoli, broken into florets
freshly ground black pepper

1   Melt butter in a large saucepan, add leeks and cook for 5 minutes or until soft. Stir in garlic, curry powder and garam masala and cook, stirring, for 1 minute longer.

2   Add barley, potatoes, pumpkin and stock or water and bring to the boil. Reduce heat, cover and simmer for 15 minutes. Add broccoli and simmer for 10 minutes longer or until barley and vegetables are tender.

Serves 4

Any vegetables you wish may be used in this dish. You might like to use carrots in place of the pumpkin, and cauliflower in place of the broccoli.

29

Right: Potato Curry in Filo Cups
Far right: Coconut Vegetable Curry

POTATO CURRY IN FILO CUPS

FILO CUPS
8 sheets filo pastry
vegetable oil

POTATO AND TOMATO CURRY
2 tablespoons vegetable oil
500 g/1 lb potatoes, cubed
1 teaspoon ground turmeric
1/2 teaspoon garam masala
1/4 teaspoon chilli powder
1 teaspoon ground coriander
1 teaspoon finely grated fresh ginger
1 large onion, chopped
1 clove garlic, crushed
4 tomatoes, peeled and chopped

To make the Filo Cups, use individual soufflé dishes 7.5-10 cm/3-4 in in diameter. The cups can be filled with a large variety of savoury or sweet foods.

1   To make Filo Cups, cut each pastry sheet in half, then each half into a 20 cm/ 8 in square. Brush sheets with oil and layer 4 sheets together. Mould gently into a greased individual soufflé dish. Repeat with remaining pastry to make 4 pastry cups and bake for 10 minutes. Remove cups from dishes and place upside down on a baking tray and bake for 5 minutes longer.

2   To make curry, heat oil in a large frying pan, add potatoes and cook, stirring, until golden. Remove potatoes from pan and set aside.

3   Add turmeric, garam masala, chilli powder, coriander, ginger, onion and garlic to pan and cook, stirring, for 5 minutes or until onion is soft. Stir in tomatoes and cook, stirring occasionally, for 15-20 minutes or until tomatoes reduce to a pulp.

4   Return potatoes to pan, cover and cook over a medium heat, stirring frequently, for 15 minutes or until potatoes are tender. Spoon curry into cups and serve immediately.

Serves 4

30

Coconut Vegetable Curry

1 tablespoon vegetable oil
1 onion, chopped
2 cloves garlic, crushed
1 teaspoon ground cumin
1 teaspoon ground coriander
1 teaspoon garam masala
$^1/_2$ teaspoon chilli powder
2 tablespoons flour
1 cup/250 mL/8 fl oz vegetable stock
or water
440 g/14 oz canned tomatoes,
undrained and mashed
2 potatoes, chopped
1 eggplant (aubergine), chopped
2 zucchini (courgettes), chopped
1 red pepper, chopped
$^1/_2$ cup/125 mL/4 fl oz coconut milk

1   Heat oil in a large frying pan, add onion and stir-fry for 5 minutes or until onion is soft. Add garlic, cumin, coriander, garam masala, chilli powder and flour and cook, stirring, for 1 minute.

2   Stir in stock or water, tomatoes and potatoes and bring to the boil. Reduce heat, cover and simmer for 15 minutes. Add eggplant (aubergine), zucchini (courgettes) and red pepper and cook for 10 minutes longer or until vegetables are tender. Stir in coconut milk and cook, stirring, for 5 minutes or until heated through.

Serves 4

Always buy spices in small quantities or the spice will have lost much of its fragrance and colour by the time you are halfway through the packet.

SIDE DISHES

*These easy side dishes will add that special
something to an otherwise simple meal. Spinach Curry
is delicious served with grilled lamb chops or pan-cooked chicken,
while the Curried Vegetable Pancakes make an interesting
change from plain potatoes. Add interest and style to
your meals with these spicy side dishes.*

Curried Vegetable
Pancakes

Pickled Ginger

Gingered Zucchini

Broccoli in Ginger
Soy Sauce

Mustard Potato Salad

Chilli Beans and Bacon

Spinach Curry

Spicy Wholemeal
Parathas

Chilli Onion Rings

Brussels Sprouts with
Mustard

Curried Vegetable Pancakes

CURRIED VEGETABLE PANCAKES

200 g/6$^{1}/_{2}$ oz pumpkin, grated
2 large potatoes, grated
1 onion, grated
$^{1}/_{2}$ cup/125 g/4 oz sour cream
$^{1}/_{2}$ cup/125 mL/4 fl oz milk
$^{1}/_{3}$ cup/45 g/1$^{1}/_{2}$ oz flour
2 teaspoons curry powder
2 eggs, lightly beaten
vegetable oil for shallow-frying

1   Place pumpkin, potatoes and onion in a colander and set over a bowl to drain. Squeeze to remove as much excess moisture as possible.

2   Place vegetables, sour cream, milk, flour, curry powder and eggs in a bowl and mix well to combine.

3   Heat oil in a large frying pan. Drop tablespoons of vegetable mixture into the hot oil and cook for 2-3 minutes each side or until golden. Drain on absorbent kitchen paper and serve immediately.

Serves 4

Carrots, turnips or parsnips can be used in place of the pumpkin in this recipe if you wish.

PICKLED GINGER

125 g/4 oz peeled fresh ginger, cut into thin slices
$^{1}/_{2}$ cup/125 mL/4 fl oz rice vinegar
2 tablespoons honey

1   Place ginger in a bowl. Pour over boiling water to cover and stand for 1 minute. Drain and set aside.

2   Place vinegar and honey in a saucepan and cook for 3-4 minutes or until honey melts and mixture is hot. Pour vinegar mixture over ginger and toss to coat. Cover and store in the refrigerator. Leave for 2-3 days before using, then use as required.

Makes 1 cup/250 mL/8 fl oz

Pickled ginger goes a pretty pink colour. Add one drop of red food colouring if you would like to intensify this effect.
Serve pickled ginger as part of a Japanese meal or as a pickle on a vegetable and cheese platter.

GINGERED ZUCCHINI

2 tablespoons vegetable oil
2 teaspoons finely grated fresh ginger
1 onion, sliced
1 clove garlic, crushed
4 zucchini (courgettes), cut into
1 cm/^{1}/$_2$ in slices
^{1}/$_4$ cup/60 mL/2 fl oz vegetable stock
or water
freshly ground black pepper
1 tablespoon snipped fresh chives

1   Heat oil in a large frying pan, add
ginger, onion and garlic and stir-fry for
1-2 minutes. Add zucchini (courgettes)
and stir-fry for 3-4 minutes longer.

2   Pour in stock or water and bring to the
boil. Reduce heat and cook until zucchini
(courgettes) are tender. Season to taste
with black pepper, sprinkle with chives
and serve immediately.

Serves 4

Carrots are also delicious
cooked in this way, but
remember that the cooking
time will be a little longer.

BROCCOLI IN GINGER SOY SAUCE

1 tablespoon vegetable oil
1 large head broccoli, broken into florets
freshly ground black pepper

GINGER SOY SAUCE
1 tablespoon soy sauce
1 tablespoon grated fresh ginger
2 teaspoons cornflour blended with
^{1}/$_2$ cup/125 mL/4 fl oz vegetable stock
or water

1   Heat oil in a wok or frying pan, add
broccoli and stir-fry for 2-3 minutes or
until broccoli changes colour.

2   To make sauce, combine soy sauce,
ginger and cornflour mixture. Pour over
broccoli in pan and cook, stirring, for 2-3
minutes or until sauce thickens. Season
to taste with black pepper and serve
immediately.

Serves 4

Fresh root ginger freezes well.
When you want to use it,
simply grate the required
amount off the piece of
frozen ginger.

*'It is said that ginger is a good remedy for, and
can even help prevent, travel sickness.'*

Broccoli in Ginger Soy Sauce,
Pickled Ginger, Gingered Zucchini

Right: Mustard Potato Salad
Far right: Chilli Beans and Bacon

MUSTARD POTATO SALAD

Mustard has been used as a
condiment since at least
Roman times. The Romans
pounded the seeds and
steeped them in wine. They
also ate the leaves as a
green vegetable. Mustard is
frequently mentioned in the
Bible and in Greek and
Roman literature.

1 kg/2 lb baby new potatoes, scrubbed

MUSTARD DRESSING
3 tablespoons sour cream
3 tablespoons mayonnaise
2 tablespoons wholegrain mustard
2 tablespoons Dijon mustard

1   Boil or microwave potatoes until
tender. Drain, refresh under cold running
water, drain again and refrigerate until
ready to serve.

2   To make dressing, place sour cream,
mayonnaise, wholegrain and Dijon
mustards in a bowl and mix to combine.
Place potatoes in a salad bowl, spoon over
dressing and serve.

Serves 6

CHILLI BEANS AND BACON

1 tablespoon olive oil
1 teaspoon chilli paste (sambal oelek)
1 onion, chopped
6 rashers bacon, chopped
440 g/14 oz canned lima or butter
beans, drained and rinsed
2 tablespoons chopped fresh parsley
freshly ground black pepper

1   Heat oil in a large frying pan, add chilli paste (sambal oelek), onion and bacon and cook, stirring constantly, for 4-5 minutes or until bacon is cooked.

2   Add beans and cook for 5 minutes longer or until heated through. Stir in parsley and season to taste with black pepper.

Serves 4

This easy vegetable dish can also be served as a main meal for two. Simply accompany with a tossed green salad and crusty bread rolls.

SPINACH CURRY

This quick Spinach Curry makes a wonderful dish for a vegetarian meal or as an accompaniment to a mild meat dish.

60 g/2 oz ghee or clarified butter
1 onion, finely chopped
2 cloves garlic, crushed
2 small fresh red chillies, finely sliced
1 teaspoon grated fresh ginger
1 bunch/500 g/1 lb spinach, stalks removed and leaves shredded
freshly ground black pepper

1   Melt ghee or butter in a frying pan, add onion, garlic, chillies and ginger and stir-fry for 5 minutes or until onion is soft.

2   Add spinach leaves, toss to coat with spices and cook for 4-5 minutes or until spinach begins to wilt. Season to taste with black pepper and serve immediately.

Serves 4

SPICY WHOLEMEAL PARATHAS

3 cups/375 g/12 oz flour
1 cup/155 g/5 oz wholemeal flour
125 g/4 oz butter
1¹/₂ cups/375 mL/12 fl oz water
250 g/8 oz mashed potato
125 g/4 oz grated tasty cheese
(mature Cheddar)
2 teaspoons curry powder
1 teaspoon ground cumin

1   Place flour and wholemeal flour in a food processor and process to sift. Add 60 g/2 oz butter and process until mixture resembles coarse breadcrumbs.

2   With machine running, add water and process to form a dough. Turn dough onto a lightly floured surface and knead for 5 minutes or until smooth. Set aside to stand for 5 minutes.

3   Place mashed potato, cheese, curry powder and cumin in a bowl and mix to combine.

4   Divide dough into twelve equal portions and press out each portion to form a 10 cm/4 in circle. Divide potato mixture between dough circles and spread evenly over dough, leaving a border around the edge. Fold dough circles in half to enclose the filling, then carefully roll again to form a 10 cm/4 in circle.

5   Melt remaining butter in a large frying pan and cook a few parathas at a time for 3-4 minutes each side or until golden and cooked through.

Makes 12

Parathas are an unleavened Indian bread. This version with a cumin-flavoured potato and cheese filling is delicious served with meat or vegetable curries.

CHILLI ONION RINGS

$^1/_2$ cup/125 mL/4 fl oz buttermilk
or milk
2 fresh red chillies, seeded and chopped
2 large onions, cut into rings
5 mm/$^1/_4$ in thick
2 cups/250 g/8 oz flour
vegetable oil for deep-frying
2 tablespoons chilli sauce or chutney

1   Place milk and chillies in a food processor or blender and process for 30 seconds. Transfer to a bowl, add onion rings and toss to coat with milk mixture.

2   Sift flour into a large bowl. Using a slotted spoon, remove onion rings from milk mixture, drain, add to bowl and coat onion rings in flour.

3   Heat oil in a large saucepan until a cube of bread dropped in browns in 50 seconds. Add a few onion rings at a time and cook for 2-3 minutes or until golden and crisp. Drain on absorbent kitchen paper and serve immediately with chilli sauce or chutney.

Serves 4

To keep cooked onion rings warm, place on absorbent kitchen paper in an ovenproof dish in an oven set at 150°C/300°F/Gas 2.

BRUSSELS SPROUTS WITH MUSTARD

500 g/1 lb Brussels sprouts

MUSTARD SAUCE
15 g/$^1/_2$ oz butter
1 tablespoon flour
$^1/_2$ cup/125 mL/4 fl oz hot milk
1 cup/250 mL/8 fl oz chicken stock
2 teaspoons wholegrain mustard
1 tablespoon mayonnaise

1   Boil, steam or microwave Brussels sprouts until just tender. Drain, set aside and keep warm.

2   To make sauce, melt butter in a saucepan, add flour and cook, stirring, for 1 minute. Remove pan from heat and whisk in milk, then stock. Return pan to heat and cook, stirring, for 4-5 minutes or until sauce boils and thickens. Stir in mustard and mayonnaise. Spoon sauce over Brussels sprouts and serve immediately.

Serves 4

Try this Mustard Sauce poured over other vegetables such as cauliflower, broccoli or zucchini (courgettes).

Brussels Sprouts with Mustard

PRESERVES

*Making your own preserves allows you to control the sweetness,
the fire or the tartness of the end result. This selection of
homemade chutneys, relishes and pickles is bound to delight the
taste buds of family and friends.*

Mint Chutney

Spicy Date Chutney

Chilli Sambal

Pickled Cabbage

Cinnamon Pears
in Brandy

Spicy Apple Chutney

Corn and Mustard
Seed Relish

Pickled Onions

*Spicy Date Chutney, Chilli Sambal,
Mint Chutney, Pickled Cabbage*

MINT CHUTNEY

125 g/4 oz fresh mint sprigs
3 fresh green chillies, seeded and chopped
3 spring onions, chopped
2 teaspoons sugar
1/2 teaspoon salt
1 tablespoon vinegar

1   Remove mint leaves from stalks. Discard stalks and wash and dry leaves.

2   Place mint leaves, chillies, spring onions, sugar, salt and vinegar in a food processor or blender and process until smooth.

3   Transfer mixture to a warm sterilised jar. Seal and label when cold. Store in the refrigerator until required.

Makes 1 x 125 g/4 oz jar

The food processor makes the preparation of this chutney very easy. The chutney will keep for up to a week in the refrigerator, and though it loses its colour after the first day or so it still tastes great.
Mint Chutney is a delicious accompaniment to an Indian meal.

SPICY DATE CHUTNEY

250 g/8 oz fresh or dried dates, pitted and chopped
1 orange, peeled and chopped
1 teaspoon grated fresh ginger
60 g/2 oz raisins
1 tablespoon brown sugar
1/3 cup/90 mL/3 fl oz cider vinegar
1/4 cup/60 mL/2 fl oz water

1   Place dates, orange, ginger, raisins, sugar, vinegar and water in a saucepan and cook over a low heat, stirring occasionally, for 20 minutes.

2   Transfer mixture to warm sterilised jars. Seal and label when cold. Store in the refrigerator until required.

Makes 2 x 250 g/8 oz jars

A delicious sweet chutney that can also be made using figs instead of dates if you wish.
Use as an accompaniment to cold meats or eat with cheese.

'The word "ginger" is from the ancient Sanskrit word singabera, *meaning "shaped like a horn".'*

CHILLI SAMBAL

25 small fresh red chillies,
stalks removed
2 cloves garlic
1 small onion, chopped
2 tablespoons brown sugar
$^3/_4$ cup/185 mL/6 fl oz water
1 teaspoon cornflour
2 tablespoons white vinegar

Use this sambal as a dipping sauce or keep a jar in the refrigerator to add some quick flavour to your recipes. When a recipe calls for chilli paste (sambal oelek) this sambal can be used.

1   Place chillies, garlic and onion in a food processor or blender and process to make a paste. Transfer to a small saucepan, stir in sugar, water, cornflour and vinegar and bring to the boil. Reduce heat and simmer until mixture thickens.

2   Remove pan from heat and set aside to cool. Transfer mixture to a warm sterilised jar. Seal and label when cold. Store in the refrigerator until required.

Makes 1 x 125 mL/4 oz jar

PICKLED CABBAGE

1 kg/2 lb Chinese cabbage,
coarsely chopped
1 tablespoon salt
2 spring onions, chopped
2 cloves garlic, crushed
1 tablespoon chilli paste (sambal oelek)
2 teaspoons grated fresh ginger
$^1/_2$ cup/125 mL/4 fl oz light soy sauce
$^1/_2$ cup/125 mL/4 fl oz white vinegar
$^1/_2$ teaspoon sesame oil

Traditional Kim Chee is made months in advance and is placed in large stone jars to mature. This simplified version is ready after one week.

1   Place cabbage in a large bowl, sprinkle with salt and set aside for 4 hours.

2   Press cabbage to remove excess liquid and drain. Add spring onions, garlic, chilli paste (sambal oelek), ginger, soy sauce and vinegar and stir to combine.

3   Pack cabbage mixture into a large warm sterilised jar and seal. Label and leave in a cool place for at least 1 week before using to allow flavours to develop. Just prior to serving, sprinkle with sesame oil.

Makes 1 x l litre/1$^3/_4$ pt jar

From left: Spicy Apple Chutney, Cinnamon Pears in Brandy, Corn and Mustard Seed Relish

CINNAMON PEARS IN BRANDY

8 small pears, peeled, halved and cored
with stems left intact
3 tablespoons lemon juice
1 cup/250 g/8 oz sugar
1½ cups/375 mL/12 fl oz water
1 cinnamon stick, broken into pieces
2 teaspoons finely grated lemon rind
3 cups/750 mL/1¼ pt brandy

1   Place pears in a large bowl, pour over lemon juice and just enough water to cover pears.

2   Place sugar and 1½ cups/375 mL/ 12 fl oz water in a large heavy-based saucepan and cook over a low heat, stirring, until sugar dissolves. Bring to the boil without stirring. Add cinnamon stick and lemon rind.

3   Drain pears, add to pan and cook over a low heat for 10-15 minutes or until pears are just tender.

4   Arrange pears in hot sterilised jars. Stir brandy into sugar syrup and pour over pears to completely cover, then seal. Label when cold and store in a cool dark place for at least 4 weeks before using.

Makes 2 x 1.5 kg/3 lb jars

These pears are a great store cupboard dessert. All they need to accompany them is some lightly whipped cream or ice cream.

SPICY APPLE CHUTNEY

2 tablespoons vegetable oil
1 clove garlic, crushed
1 teaspoon grated fresh ginger
2 fresh red chillies, seeded and chopped
2 tablespoons mustard seeds
1 teaspoon mixed spice
1 teaspoon ground turmeric
15 whole black peppercorns
2 teaspoons ground cumin
8 large cooking apples, cored, peeled
and sliced
$^2/_3$ cup/170 mL/5$^1/_2$ fl oz white vinegar
$^1/_2$ cup/125 g/4 oz sugar

1 Heat oil in a large saucepan, add garlic, ginger and chillies and cook over a medium heat for 2-3 minutes. Stir in mustard seeds, mixed spice, turmeric, peppercorns and cumin and cook for 3-4 minutes longer.

2 Add apples, vinegar and sugar to pan, bring to simmering and simmer, uncovered, for 1 hour or until chutney is thick. Spoon chutney into hot sterilised jars and seal and label when cold.

Makes 2 x 250 g/8 oz jars

To sterilise jars, wash in hot water then warm in the oven at a low temperature until dry. Remember that the lids must also be sterilised.

CORN AND MUSTARD SEED RELISH

1 large onion, chopped
2 cups/500 mL/16 fl oz white
wine vinegar
$^1/_2$ cup/100 g/3$^1/_2$ oz caster sugar
1 tablespoon curry powder
1 teaspoon ground turmeric
2 teaspoons yellow mustard seeds
2 tablespoons grated fresh ginger
2 x 440 g/14 oz canned sweet corn
kernels, drained
1 carrot, finely chopped
2 stalks celery, chopped
1 red pepper, chopped
2 tablespoons cornflour blended with
$^1/_2$ cup/125 mL/4 fl oz water
freshly ground black pepper

1 Place onion in a small saucepan and pour over enough water just to cover. Bring to the boil, then remove from heat, drain and set aside.

2 Place vinegar, sugar, curry powder, turmeric, mustard seeds and ginger in a large saucepan and bring to the boil. Reduce heat and simmer for 3-4 minutes.

3 Stir in sweet corn kernels, carrot, celery, red pepper and onion and bring back to the boil. Reduce heat and simmer for 15 minutes. Stir in cornflour mixture and cook over a medium heat, stirring constantly, for 5 minutes or until mixture boils and thickens. Season to taste with black pepper. Spoon relish into hot sterilised jars. Seal and label when cold. Store in a cool dark place until required.

Makes 3 x 250 g/8 oz jars

Preserves should be covered either immediately after potting or when completely cold. Never cover when just warm, as this creates conditions ideal for the growth of mould. If you are going to allow the preserve to cool before covering, place a clean cloth over the jars to prevent dust falling on the surface of the contents.

PICKLED ONIONS

2 kg/4 lb pickling onions, unpeeled
750 g/1^1/$_2$ lb salt

PICKLING VINEGAR
6 cups/1.5 litres/2^1/$_2$ pt white wine
vinegar
1 tablespoon salt
2 teaspoons ground ginger
6 whole cloves
2 fresh red chillies, cut in half
2 teaspoons yellow mustard seeds
6 whole black peppercorns
2 bay leaves

1   Place onions and 750 g/1^1/$_2$ lb salt in a bowl. Add enough water to cover onions and set aside to stand for 2 days. Stir occasionally during standing time.

2   Drain onions and discard liquid. Peel onions, place in a bowl and pour over boiling water to cover. Set aside to stand for 3 minutes, then drain and repeat twice more using additional boiling water. Pack onions into hot sterilised jars and set aside.

3   To make vinegar, place white wine vinegar, 1 tablespoon salt, ginger, cloves, chillies, mustard seeds, peppercorns and bay leaves in a large saucepan and bring to the boil. Reduce heat and simmer for 10 minutes. Remove pan from heat and set aside to cool slightly, then pour liquid over onions in jars and seal. Label when cold and store in a cool dark place for 2 months before using.

Makes 2 x 1.5 kg/3 lb jars

Remember jars should be warm when adding the hot preserve. Cold jars may crack or break if a hot mixture is suddenly added to them.

'Cloves were so highly regarded by the people of the Spice Islands that they planted a clove tree on the birth of a child. It was believed that if the tree flourished then so would the child.'

BAKED GOODS

The sweet spices, such as cinnamon, cloves, nutmeg and cardamom, are the ones most used in baking. This selection of cakes, biscuits and slices shows just how important spices are in baking. Although most recipes have only a teaspoon or two of spice, this is enough to add a characteristic taste and aroma.

Spiced Cherry Cake

Sugar and Spice
Biscuits

Apricot Pie

Cherry Pie

Apple Pie

Pumpkin and Rum Tart

Country Apple Flan

Chelsea Bun

Sultana Pikelets

Nutmeg Fruit Loaf

Shortbread Swirls

Spiced Ginger Drops

Gingerbread Cake

Ginger Crunch

Spiced Cherry Cake

SPICED CHERRY CAKE

125 g/4 oz butter
1 cup/170 g/5^1/2 oz brown sugar
3 eggs
1 cup/125 g/4 oz flour
1 cup/125 g/4 oz self-raising flour
^{1}/2 teaspoon bicarbonate of soda
2 teaspoons mixed spice
1 cup/315 g/10 oz cherry jam
^{1}/3 cup/90 mL/3 fl oz buttermilk or milk

Makes a 23 cm/9 in ring cake

1   Place butter and sugar in a bowl and beat until light and fluffy. Add eggs one at a time, beating well after each addition.

2   Sift together flour, self-raising flour, bicarbonate of soda and mixed spice. Place jam and milk in bowl and mix to combine. Fold flour mixture and jam mixture, alternately, into butter mixture and mix well to combine.

3   Spoon batter into a well-greased 23 cm/9 in ring tin and bake for 45 minutes or until cooked when tested with a skewer. Stand in tin for 5 minutes before turning onto a wire rack to cool completely.

Oven temperature
180°C, 350°F, Gas 4

Mixed spice should not be confused with allspice, which is a spice in its own right. Mixed spice, as the name suggests, is a mixture of spices which includes cinnamon, cloves, nutmeg and allspice. The exact spices used, and the proportions, vary according to the brand.

SUGAR AND SPICE BISCUITS

2 cups/250 g/8 oz flour
^{1}/2 teaspoon ground cinnamon
^{1}/4 teaspoon ground allspice
^{1}/4 teaspoon ground mace
^{1}/4 teaspoon ground cloves
^{1}/2 teaspoon baking powder
^{1}/2 cup/125 g/4 oz sugar
125 g/4 oz butter
1 egg, lightly beaten

SUGAR GLAZE
1 egg, lightly beaten
1 tablespoon milk
2 teaspoons caster sugar
2 tablespoons sugar

1   Place flour, cinnamon, allspice, mace, cloves, baking powder and sugar in a food processor or blender and process to combine. Add butter and process until mixture resembles fine breadcrumbs.

With machine running, slowly add egg and process to form a soft dough.

2   Turn dough onto a lightly floured surface and knead briefly. Roll out dough to 3 mm/^{1}/8 in thick and using fancy biscuit cutters cut out as many shapes as possible. Place biscuits on greased baking trays. Knead trimmings, reroll and cut out more shapes to make 32 in total. Refrigerate biscuits for 30 minutes.

3   To make glaze, place egg, milk and caster sugar in a small bowl and mix to combine. Just prior to baking, brush biscuits with glaze, then bake for 15-20 minutes or until lightly browned. Remove biscuits from oven and sprinkle with sugar. Allow biscuits to stand on trays for 3 minutes before transferring to wire racks to cool completely.

Makes 32

Oven temperature
180°C, 350°F, Gas 4

Allspice is the aromatic berry of the pimento tree. The French call it *quatre-épices* (four spices) as to them the flavour seems to suggest a combination of cinnamon, cloves, pepper and nutmeg. It is an important ingredient in the spice mixture sold as mixed spice.
Most of the world's supply of allspice is still grown in Jamaica.

APRICOT PIE

Oven temperature
200°C, 400°F, Gas 6

Cinnamon is the dried bark of a tree belonging to the laurel family. It is available as quills (sticks) or ground. Quills are the longest and best pieces of the bark which are rolled by hand, then dried until they are tan in colour and smooth, thin and brittle.

250 g/8 oz prepared shortcrust pastry

APRICOT FILLING
3 x 440 g/14 oz canned apricot halves, drained and sliced
$^1/4$ cup/45 g/$1^1/2$ oz brown sugar
$^1/2$ teaspoon ground nutmeg
$^1/2$ teaspoon ground cinnamon

1 To make filling, place apricots, sugar, nutmeg and cinnamon in a bowl and mix to combine.

2 Spoon filling into a greased 23 cm/9 in pie plate. Roll out pastry to 3 mm/$^1/8$ in thick. Mark centre of pastry and cut four 10 cm/4 in slits, crossing in the centre. Place pastry over filling and trim edges 5 mm/$^1/4$ in wider than rim of plate. Fold back flaps of pastry from centre of pie. Make a large scalloped edge by placing your thumb against the inside pastry edge and moulding the pastry around it with fingers of other hand.

3 Bake pie for 20-30 minutes or until pastry is golden and cooked through.

Serves 6

CHERRY PIE

Oven temperature
220°C, 425°F, Gas 7

The *Myristica fragrans* tree produces two spices – nutmeg and mace. Nutmeg is the kernel of the seed while mace is the lacy covering that surrounds the seed. The fruit of the tree looks somewhat like an apricot. When it matures it splits, exposing the aril or mace. This is removed and dried until it is a tan colour. The nutmeg is dried separately.

375 g/12 oz prepared shortcrust pastry

CHERRY FILLING
3 x 440 g/14 oz canned pitted black cherries
2 tablespoons brown sugar
1 tablespoon flour
1 teaspoon ground mixed spice

1 To make filling, drain cherries on sheets of absorbent kitchen paper. Place cherries, sugar, flour and mixed spice in a bowl and mix to combine.

2 Roll out two-thirds of the pastry to 3 mm/$^1/8$ in thick and line a greased 23 cm/9 in pie dish. Spoon filling into pastry case. Roll out remaining pastry and, using a pastry cutter, cut into 2 cm/$^3/4$ in wide strips. Twist each strip and arrange in a lattice pattern over filling. Brush edge of pie with a little water and seal each strip to edge.

3 Bake pie for 20 minutes, then reduce temperature to 160°C/325°F/Gas 3 and bake for 30-40 minutes longer or until pastry is golden and cooked through.

Serves 6

Apple Pie

500 g/1 lb prepared shortcrust pastry

APPLE FILLING
2 x 440 g/14 oz canned sliced apples
$^{1}/_{4}$ cup/60 g/2 oz sugar
$^{1}/_{2}$ teaspoon ground cloves
$^{1}/_{2}$ teaspoon ground cardamom

1   To make filling, place apples, sugar, cloves and cardamom in a bowl and mix to combine.

2   Roll out two-thirds of the pastry to 3 mm/$^{1}/_{8}$ in thick and line a greased 23 cm/9 in pie dish. Spoon filling into pastry shell.

3   Roll out remaining pastry to make a 25 cm/10 in circle. Cut out apple shapes as shown in picture. Brush pastry with a little water and place apple shapes between cut-out shapes. Place pastry circle over filling, trim edge and fold under bottom pastry layer. To form rope edge, pinch edge at a slant using your thumb and index finger and at the same time pulling back with thumb.

4   Bake pie for 20 minutes, then reduce temperature to 160°C/325°F/Gas 3 and cook for 30-40 minutes longer or until pastry is golden and cooked through.

Serves 6

Oven temperature
220°C, 425°F, Gas 7

Cardamom is the third most expensive spice after saffron and vanilla; it is also one of the most ancient spices. In India its economic importance is such that it is known as 'the queen of spices', second only to pepper 'the king'.

Apple Pie

PUMPKIN AND RUM TART

Oven temperature
200°C, 400°F, Gas 6

PASTRY
1^1/$_2$ cups/185 g/6 oz flour
90 g/3 oz butter
2-3 tablespoons cold water

PUMPKIN FILLING
300 g/9^1/$_2$ oz pumpkin, cooked
and mashed
1 cup/250 mL/8 fl oz evaporated milk
3 eggs, beaten
1 cup/170 g/5^1/$_2$ oz brown sugar
1 teaspoon mixed spice
1 teaspoon ground ginger
^{1}/$_4$ cup/60 mL/2 fl oz dark rum

1 To make pastry, place flour in a food processor and process to sift. Add butter and process until mixture resembles fine breadcrumbs. With machine running, slowly add water to form a soft dough. Turn pastry onto a lightly floured surface and knead briefly. Roll out pastry to 3 mm/^{1}/$_8$ in thick and line a lightly greased 23 cm/9 in flan tin. Line pastry case with nonstick baking paper, weigh down with uncooked rice and bake for 10-15 minutes. Remove rice and paper and cook for 5-10 minutes longer or until pastry is golden.

2 To make filling, place pumpkin, milk, eggs, sugar, mixed spice, ginger and rum in a bowl and mix well to combine. Pour filling into pastry case, reduce oven temperature to 180°C/350°F/Gas 4 and bake for 40 minutes or until filling is firm.

Serves 8

This tart is delicious served warm or cold with cream or ice cream.

COUNTRY APPLE FLAN

Left: Pumpkin and Rum Tart
Above: Country Apple Flan

³/4 teaspoon dried yeast
³/4 cup/185 mL/6 fl oz warm water
1¹/2 cups/185 g/6 oz flour, sifted
¹/4 teaspoon salt

APPLE HONEY FILLING
2 tablespoons honey, melted
3 green apples, cored, peeled and thinly sliced
2 teaspoons cinnamon sugar
2 tablespoons brown sugar

1   Dissolve yeast in water and stand in a warm, draught-free place for 5 minutes or until frothy.

2   Place flour and salt in a large bowl, make a well in the centre of mixture, pour in yeast mixture and gradually stir in flour. Mix to form a dough. Turn dough onto a lightly floured surface and knead for 10 minutes or until dough is smooth and elastic. Place dough in a greased bowl, cover with plastic food wrap and set aside to stand in a warm, draught-free place for 1 hour or until doubled in size. Punch dough down, cover with plastic food wrap and set aside to rise again for 30 minutes.

3   Roll out dough to fit a 23 cm/9 in flan tin. Line pastry case with nonstick baking paper, weigh down with uncooked rice and bake for 15 minutes.

4   Remove rice and paper from pastry case and brush with honey. Arrange apple slices in pastry case, sprinkle with cinnamon and brown sugar and bake for 30 minutes.

Serves 6

Oven temperature
180°C, 350°F, Gas 4

Cinnamon sugar is simply a mixture of ground cinnamon and caster sugar. You can purchase it in the spice section of the supermarket or make it yourself. To make, mix ¹/4 cup/60 g/2 oz caster sugar with 1-2 teaspoons ground cinnamon.

CHELSEA BUN

Oven temperature
180°C, 350°F, Gas 4

2 cups/250 g/8 oz self-raising flour
1 teaspoon baking powder
2 teaspoons sugar
45 g/1^1/$_2$ oz butter
1 egg
^{1}/$_2$ cup/125 mL/4 fl oz milk

FRUIT FILLING
60 g/2 oz butter, softened
4 tablespoons brown sugar
1 teaspoon ground mixed spice
250 g/8 oz mixed dried fruit

SUGAR GLAZE
1 tablespoon water
1 tablespoon sugar
1 teaspoon gelatine

1 Sift together flour and baking powder into a large bowl. Stir in sugar, then rub in butter using fingertips until mixture resembles coarse breadcrumbs.

2 Whisk together egg and milk. Make a well in the centre of the flour mixture and pour in egg mixture. Mix to form a soft dough, turn onto a floured surface and knead lightly. Roll out dough on a lightly floured surface to form a 20 x 30 cm/8 x 12 in rectangle.

3 To make filling, place butter, brown sugar and mixed spice in a bowl and beat until smooth. Spread butter mixture over dough, then sprinkle with mixed fruit. Roll up lengthwise and cut into eight thick slices, using a sharp knife. Arrange slices over the base of a greased, shallow 20 cm/8 in cake tin and bake for 25-30 minutes or until golden.

4 To make glaze, place water, sugar and gelatine in a saucepan and cook over a low heat, stirring constantly, until sugar and gelatine dissolve. Brush hot bun with glaze. Serve warm or cold.

Serves 6

Dried and ground spices should be stored in sealed containers at room temperature in a cool dark place. Heat, light and moisture all affect the quality of spices. If stored correctly, ground spices will keep fresh for six months, while whole spices can keep for as long as a year.

Chelsea Bun, Nutmeg Fruit Loaf, Sultana Pikelets

SULTANA PIKELETS

1 cup/125 g/4 oz flour
1 teaspoon baking powder
1 teaspoon mixed spice
3 tablespoons caster sugar
3 tablespoons chopped sultanas
1 egg, lightly beaten
$^1\!/_2$ cup/125 mL/4 fl oz milk
4 tablespoons cream

1 Sift together flour, baking powder and mixed spice into a large bowl. Stir in sugar and sultanas, then make a well in the centre of mixture.

2 Place egg, milk and cream in a small bowl and whisk to combine. Gradually stir egg mixture into dry ingredients and mix until batter is smooth.

3 Cook dessertspoonfuls of mixture in a heated, greased, heavy-based frying pan until bubbles appear on the surface, then turn and cook until golden brown.

Makes 20 pikelets

For a special occasion, top these pikelets with lightly whipped cream and jam.

NUTMEG FRUIT LOAF

Oven temperature
180°C, 350°F, Gas 4

315 g/10 oz mixed dried fruit
1 cup/250 mL/8 fl oz water
2 teaspoons ground nutmeg
125 g/4 oz butter
$^1/_2$ cup/125 g/4 oz sugar
1 egg
2 cups/250 g/8 oz self-raising flour
$^1/_2$ teaspoon baking powder
125 g/4 oz walnuts, roughly chopped

1 Place fruit, water and nutmeg in a large saucepan, bring to the boil and boil for 3 minutes. Remove pan from heat and set aside to cool.

2 Place butter and sugar in a bowl and beat until light and creamy. Add egg and continue to beat until well combined. Sift together flour and baking powder. Mix flour mixture and undrained fruit mixture, alternately, into butter mixture. Fold in walnuts.

3 Spoon batter into a greased and lined 11 x 21 cm/4$^1/_2$ x 8$^1/_2$ in loaf tin and bake for 1$^1/_4$ hours or until golden and cooked when tested with a skewer. Stand in tin for 5 minutes before turning onto a wire rack to cool completely.

Makes an 11 x 21 cm/4$^1/_2$ x 8$^1/_2$ in loaf

For the best flavour it is best to buy whole nutmegs and to grate them as required. In the eighteenth century, special folding nutmeg graters were carried by both men and women; the nutmeg was used medicinally and to flavour mulled wine.

SHORTBREAD SWIRLS

Oven temperature
190°C, 375°F, Gas 5

125 g/4 oz butter, chopped
$^3/_4$ cup/125 g/4 oz icing sugar
1$^1/_2$ cups/185 g/6 oz flour
$^1/_3$ cup/90 g/3 oz sour cream
1 teaspoon vanilla essence
3 teaspoons water

1 Place butter, icing sugar, flour, sour cream, vanilla essence and water in a food processor and process until smooth.

2 Spoon mixture into a piping bag fitted with a large star nozzle and pipe small swirls of mixture onto greased baking trays. Bake for 10-12 minutes or until lightly golden. Allow biscuits to cool on baking trays.

Makes 40

Vanilla is the dried pod of a type of orchid native to South America. You should be aware that what is often labelled as vanilla essence is not in fact vanilla at all but a synthetic product made from clove oil. When buying vanilla essence look for pure vanilla. It is more expensive but the flavour is well worth the extra cost.

Spiced Ginger Drops

SPICED GINGER DROPS

1 cup/125 g/4 oz flour, sifted
$^1/_4$ teaspoon ground ginger
$^1/_4$ teaspoon mixed spice
$^1/_4$ teaspoon ground cinnamon
$^1/_2$ teaspoon bicarbonate of soda
60 g/2 oz butter, cut into pieces
$^1/_2$ cup/90 g/3 oz brown sugar
2$^1/_2$ tablespoons golden syrup, warmed
1$^1/_2$ tablespoons finely chopped glacé
ginger or stem ginger in syrup

1   Place flour, ground ginger, mixed spice, cinnamon and bicarbonate of soda in a large mixing bowl. Rub in butter until mixture resembles fine breadcrumbs. Stir in sugar, golden syrup and glacé or stem ginger.

2   Turn dough onto a lightly floured surface and knead to form a soft dough. Roll rounded teaspoons of mixture into balls and place 3 cm/1$^1/_4$ in apart on greased baking trays. Bake for 10-15 minutes or until golden. Transfer biscuits to wire racks to cool.

Makes 30

Oven temperature
180°C, 350°F, Gas 4

Stem ginger, also known as preserved or Chinese ginger, is the tender young roots which have been cleaned and peeled then simmered in a syrup. It is often sold in pretty Chinese jars and given as gifts at Christmas.

GINGERBREAD CAKE

125 g/4 oz butter, melted
¹/2 cup/125 mL/4 fl oz hot water
¹/2 cup/170 g/5¹/2 oz golden syrup, warmed
1 cup/125 g/4 oz flour, sifted
¹/2 cup/60 g/2 oz self-raising flour, sifted
¹/2 teaspoon bicarbonate of soda
4 teaspoons ground ginger
¹/2 teaspoon ground nutmeg
¹/2 cup/90 g/3 oz brown sugar

LEMON ICING
1¹/2 cups/220 g/7¹/2 oz icing sugar, sifted
15 g/¹/2 oz butter, softened
2 teaspoons lemon juice
milk
2 tablespoons desiccated coconut

1   Place butter, water and golden syrup in a large bowl. Sift in flour, self-raising flour, bicarbonate of soda, ginger, nutmeg and sugar and mix to combine all ingredients.

2   Spoon batter into a greased 20 cm/ 8 in ring cake tin and bake for 35-40 minutes or until cake is cooked when tested with a skewer. Stand cake in tin for 5 minutes before turning onto a wire rack to cool.

3   To make icing, place icing sugar in a bowl, mix in butter, lemon juice and enough milk to make an icing of spreadable consistency. Spread icing over cold cake and sprinkle with coconut.

Makes a 20 cm/8 in ring cake

For an easy dessert, serve this Gingerbread Cake warm without the icing and accompany with custard, cream or ice cream.

GINGER CRUNCH

125 g/4 oz butter
³/4 cup/185 g/6 oz sugar
¹/2 cup/125 mL/4 fl oz sweetened condensed milk
1 tablespoon golden syrup
250 g/8 oz gingernut biscuits, crushed
60 g/2 oz pecans or walnuts, finely chopped
2 tablespoons finely chopped glacé ginger or stem ginger in syrup

1   Place butter, sugar, condensed milk and golden syrup in a small saucepan and cook over a medium heat, stirring constantly, until mixture is smooth. Bring to the boil, then reduce heat and simmer for 3-4 minutes or until mixture thickens slightly.

2   Place biscuits, pecans or walnuts and glacé or stem ginger in a bowl, pour in condensed milk mixture and mix until well combined. Press mixture into a lined, shallow 23 cm/9 in square cake tin and refrigerate until set. Cut into bars.

Makes 30

This easy-to-make slice is the perfect treat for office and school lunches.

Gingerbread Cake, Ginger Crunch,
Shortbread Swirls

DESSERTS

*All of these wonderful hot desserts rely on a touch of
spice for flavour. As with baked goods, the sweet spices really
come into their own in these end-of-meal treats.*

Walnut and Spice
Pudding

Waffles with Maple
Sauce

Pear and Cinnamon
Cake

Fruit Bread Pudding

Walnut and Spice Pudding

Walnut and Spice Pudding

75 g/2 1/2 oz butter
1/2 cup/90 g/3 oz brown sugar
1 egg
1 cup/125 g/4 oz self-raising flour, sifted
1 teaspoon ground ginger
1/4 teaspoon ground nutmeg
1/2 teaspoon ground cinnamon
1/4 teaspoon ground cloves
1/4 cup/60 mL/2 fl oz milk
4 tablespoons chopped walnuts

1   Place butter and sugar in a bowl and beat until light and fluffy. Beat in egg, then flour, ginger, nutmeg, cinnamon and cloves. Stir in milk and walnuts and mix well to combine.

2   Spoon batter into a greased 4 cup/ 1 litre/1 3/4 pt pudding basin, cover basin with foil, then place in a baking dish with 4 cm/1 1/2 in boiling water in the base. Bake for 1 1/2-1 3/4 hours or until pudding is cooked when tested with a skewer. Allow pudding to stand in basin for 10 minutes before turning out and serving.

Serves 4

Oven temperature
180°C, 350°F, Gas 4

Cloves are the unopened flower buds of a tree native to the Spice Islands.
An orange studded with cloves, rubbed with orris root and tied with a pretty ribbon makes a fragrant pomander for scenting a wardrobe.

Waffles with Maple Sauce

8 prepared waffles, heated

MAPLE SAUCE
2/3 cup/170 mL/5 1/2 fl oz maple syrup
4 tablespoons honey
1/2 teaspoon ground allspice
1 teaspoon ground cinnamon
pinch caraway seeds

1   To make sauce, place maple syrup and honey in a small heavy-based saucepan and cook over a low heat, stirring, for 5 minutes or until honey melts and mixture is hot.

2   Stir in allspice, cinnamon and caraway seeds. Spoon sauce over waffles and serve immediately.

Serves 4

The Maple Sauce is also delicious over pancakes, bananas or ice cream.

PEAR AND CINNAMON CAKE

Oven temperature
180°C, 350°F, Gas 4

250 g/8 oz butter, softened
1 cup/170 g/5^1/$_2$ oz brown sugar
4 eggs
2 cups/250 g/8 oz self-raising flour,
sifted
3 teaspoons ground cinnamon
5 canned pear halves, drained and sliced
3 tablespoons sugar

Canned apricots, peaches
or apples could also be used
to make this dessert. If using
apples or apricots you might
like to replace the cinnamon
with nutmeg.

1 Place butter and brown sugar in a
large bowl and beat until light and fluffy.
Beat in eggs one at a time, beating well
after each addition. Add flour and 2
teaspoons cinnamon and beat well to
combine.

2 Spoon batter into a greased and lined
23 cm/9 in cake tin. Arrange pear slices
attractively on top of batter. Combine
sugar and remaining cinnamon, sprinkle
over top of cake and bake for 1^1/$_4$-1^1/$_2$
hours or until cake is cooked when tested
with a skewer.

Serves 8

FRUIT BREAD PUDDING

Oven temperature
180°C, 350°F, Gas 4

15 thick slices fruit bread
125 g/4 oz butter, melted
3 eggs
3 cups/750 mL/1^1/$_4$ pt milk
^{3}/$_4$ cup/125 g/4 oz icing sugar
2 teaspoons vanilla essence
1 teaspoon ground nutmeg
3 teaspoons ground cinnamon
2 tablespoons caster sugar

This is the easiest bread
pudding you will ever make.
It takes only minutes to
prepare and cooks while you
are eating the main course.

1 Cut each slice of bread into nine
squares and place in a large bowl. Pour
over melted butter and toss to coat.
Transfer bread to a greased baking dish.

2 Place eggs, milk, icing sugar, vanilla
essence, nutmeg and 2 teaspoons
cinnamon in a bowl and whisk to
combine. Strain egg mixture through a
sieve, then carefully pour over bread.
Sprinkle with caster sugar and remaining
cinnamon and bake for 30 minutes.

Serves 6

Pear and Cinnamon Cake,
Fruit Bread Pudding

SPICE MIXES

The secret of many dishes is a combination of spices. Many of these are available ready-made, but nothing can compare with the fresh taste of homemade curry powder or your own harissa. The big advantage of making your own spice mixes is that you can alter the proportions of ingredients to suit your taste and requirements.

GARAM MASALA

10 green or 6 black cardamoms, pods
cracked and seeds removed
1 tablespoon black peppercorns
2 teaspoons cumin seeds
$^{1}/_{2}$ teaspoon coriander seeds
2 small dried red chillies, seeded

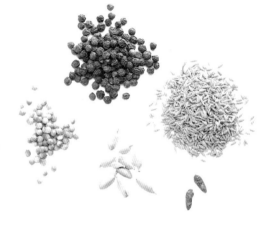

Garam masala is a popular mixture of ground spices used extensively in Indian cooking. It is available ready-made, but if you cannot get it you can easily make it yourself. Just vary the amounts of the ingredients according to personal taste.

Place cardamom seeds, black peppercorns, cumin seeds, coriander seeds and chillies in a grinder and process until finely ground. Store in an airtight container for up to 3 months.

CURRY POWDER

2 tablespoons cumin seeds
2 tablespoons fenugreek
$1^{1}/_{2}$ tablespoons mustard seeds
1 tablespoon black peppercorns
8 tablespoons coriander seeds
1 tablespoon poppy seeds
1 tablespoon ground ginger
$1^{1}/_{2}$ teaspoons hot chilli powder
4 tablespoons ground turmeric

Curry powder can be purchased in any supermarket; however, making your own is easy and adds a very special taste to any dish.

Place cumin seeds, fenugreek, mustard seeds, black peppercorns, coriander seeds and poppy seeds in a grinder and process until finely ground. Add ginger, chilli powder and turmeric and process to combine. Store in an airtight container away from direct light for up to 3 months.

FIVE SPICE POWDER

5 teaspoons ground anise
5 teaspoons star anise
12.5 cm/5 in cinnamon stick
6 teaspoons cloves
7 teaspoons fennel seeds

Five spice powder is a favourite ingredient in Chinese cooking. It adds a subtle anise flavour to Oriental dishes.

Place ground anise, star anise, cinnamon, cloves and fennel seeds in a grinder and process until finely ground. Store in an airtight container away from direct light for up to 3 months.

HARISSA

30 g/1 oz dried red chillies
1 clove garlic, chopped
1 teaspoon caraway seeds
1 teaspoon cumin seeds
1 teaspoon coriander seeds
$^{1}/_{4}$ teaspoon salt
olive oil

1   Place chillies in a small bowl, pour over enough hot water to cover and set aside to soak for 1 hour. Drain and pat dry with absorbent kitchen paper.

2   Place chillies, garlic, caraway seeds cumin seeds, coriander seeds and salt in a grinder and process to make a smooth paste. Place in a small jar, cover with olive oil, cover, label and store in the refrigerator for up to 2 months.

A coffee grinder is ideal for grinding spices, but do not use the same grinder as you use for coffee as the flavours will mix.

'The traditional pestle and mortar is also great for grinding spices and spice mixtures.'

BRANDY SNAPS

125 g/4 oz butter
³/4 cup/125 g/4 oz brown sugar
4 tablespoons golden syrup
1 tablespoon lemon juice
1 tablespoon brandy
1 cup/125 g/4 oz flour
1 teaspoon ground ginger

SPICED CREAM FILLING
1 cup/250 mL/8 fl oz cream (double)
3 tablespoons brandy
3 tablespoons icing sugar
¹/2 teaspoon ground cinnamon
or nutmeg

2 Drop well-spaced teaspoonfuls of mixture onto a well-greased baking tray and bake for 8-10 minutes or until lightly browned.

1 Place butter, brown sugar, golden syrup, lemon juice and brandy in a saucepan and cook over a medium heat, stirring constantly, until butter melts and sugar dissolves. Remove pan from heat, sift in flour and ginger and mix well to combine.

3 Remove Brandy Snaps from oven and loosen from tray with a palette knife, then wrap around oiled chopsticks or the handles of wooden spoons. Set aside and when firm remove chopsticks or spoons.

4 To make filling, place cream, brandy, icing sugar and cinnamon or nutmeg in a bowl and beat until soft peaks form. Pipe mixture into cold Brandy Snaps and serve immediately.

Makes 30

For ease of handling, bake only six Brandy Snaps at a time at 5-minute intervals and remember to have the chopsticks or wooden spoons ready.

If the Brandy Snaps become too firm to roll, simply return them to the oven for a few minutes.

Brandy Snaps

MINCEMEAT

250 g/8 oz raisins
250 g/8 oz currants
125 g/4 oz mixed peel
2 cooking apples, cored, peeled
and chopped
1 teaspoon finely grated lemon rind
1 teaspoon finely grated orange rind
$^3/_4$ cup/125 g/4 oz brown sugar
125 g/4 oz butter, melted
$^1/_2$ teaspoon ground nutmeg
$^1/_2$ teaspoon ground cinnamon
$^1/_4$ teaspoon ground cloves
$^2/_3$ cup/170 mL/5$^1/_2$ fl oz brandy

1   Finely chop raisins, currants and mixed peel and place in a large bowl.

2   Add apples, lemon rind, orange rind, sugar, butter, nutmeg, cinnamon, cloves and brandy to bowl and mix well to combine. Cover with plastic food wrap and set aside in a cool place to mature for 3 days. Stir twice a day.

3   Spoon fruit mixture into sterilised jars and cover. Store in the refrigerator for 2 weeks before using.

Makes 6 cups/1.5 kg/3 lb

MINCE PIES

prepared mincemeat (purchased, or see
recipe opposite to make your own)
icing sugar (optional)

SHORTCRUST PASTRY
1¾ cups/220 g/7 oz flour
1 tablespoon sugar
155 g/5 oz butter, chopped
1 egg yolk, lightly beaten
2 tablespoons cold water

1   To make pastry, place flour and sugar
in a large bowl. Using two knives cut in
butter until mixture resembles coarse
breadcrumbs. Mix in egg yolk and enough
water to form a firm dough. Turn onto a
lightly floured surface and knead. Wrap
pastry in plastic food wrap and refrigerate
for 1 hour.

2   Roll out pastry to 5 mm/¼ in thick
and, using a 7.5 cm/3 in biscuit cutter, cut
out 10 circles. Then, using a 4 cm/1½ in
biscuit cutter, cut out another 10 circles.
Place larger pastry circles in lightly
greased patty tins and fill with
mincemeat. Dampen smaller pastry
circles with water, place over mincemeat
and press edges to seal.

3   Using a fork, pierce tops of pies and
bake for 20 minutes or until pastry is
golden and cooked. Remove pies from
pans and serve immediately or transfer to
wire racks to cool. Just prior to serving,
sprinkle with icing sugar, if desired.

Makes 10

Oven temperature
190°C, 375°F, Gas 5

Mince pies have been
associated with Christmas
since Tudor times. Originally
they were a mixture of
minced or shredded meat,
dried fruits and spices. By the
end of the nineteenth
century the meat was
omitted and the mince pie
as we know it today was
born.

GINGERBREAD FAMILY

Oven temperature
180°C, 350°F, Gas 4

125 g/4 oz butter
$^1/_2$ cup/90 g/3 oz brown sugar
1 egg
1 cup/125 g/4 oz flour
$1^1/_2$ cups/185 g/6 oz self-raising flour
1 teaspoon bicarbonate of soda
1 tablespoon ground ginger
2 tablespoons honey

ROYAL ICING
1 egg white
$1^1/_2$ cups/250 g/8 oz icing sugar, sifted
a little lemon juice
food colouring

Freezer bags are an easy
and economical alternative
to using piping bags and
nozzles when you are using
small quantities of many
different colours.

1   Place butter and sugar in a bowl and
beat until light and fluffy. Beat in egg.
Sift together flour, self-raising flour,
bicarbonate of soda and ginger and fold
into butter mixture. Add honey and mix
well to combine.

2   Turn dough onto a lightly floured
surface and knead until soft but not sticky.
Wrap dough in plastic food wrap and
refrigerate for 30 minutes. Divide dough
into four equal portions and roll out each
portion to 3 mm/$^1/_8$ in thick.

Remember that gingerbread
becomes crisp as it cools, so
avoid overcooking.

3   Cut out shapes with gingerbread
cookie cutters or make cardboard
templates. Cut two large shapes (mother
and father) and two small shapes
(children). Using a spatula, carefully lift
gingerbread figures onto a lightly greased
baking tray. Reroll remaining dough
scraps and use to make a cat and a dog.
Place cat and dog on baking tray. Bake
for 10 minutes or until cooked. Allow
gingerbread to cool on trays.

4   To make icing, place egg white in a
bowl and beat with a wooden spoon. Add
icing sugar a tablespoon at a time, beating
well after each addition. When icing
reaches piping consistency, stir in a few
drops of lemon juice, then divide into
small quantities and colour as desired.

5 Spoon icing into small freezer bags and snip off one corner, then pipe facial features and clothes onto gingerbread shapes.

Makes a family of four plus a cat and a dog

Gingerbread Family

An A to Z of Spices

1 **ALLSPICE**: The seeds of allspice are slightly larger than peppercorns and dark brown in colour. Allspice is a delicately spicy mingling of cloves, cinnamon and nutmeg, with cloves predominating. Allspice berries are the dried fruit of a tall, aromatic evergreen of the myrtle and clove family, which can grow to over 12 m/36 ft. Picked when green and unripe, the berries are dried in the sun to a rich, deep brown colour.

2 **ANISE**: Commonly called aniseed, the small, oval grey-green ribbed seeds of anise have a warm, sweet, pungent flavour and can be used in sweet and savoury dishes. The aromatic anise annual grows to about 60 cm/2 ft high and, like parsley, is similar to other small members of the same plant family. Anise will grow well in a good summer in light, dry loamy soil in a sunny position. Sow the seeds in mid-spring. The plants produce small white flowers and fern-like leaves.

3 **CARAWAY**: A handsome biennial to 60 cm/2 ft high with finely cut leaves and clusters of white flowers which produce aromatic seeds with a characteristic flavour. Sow seeds in spring or autumn. Needs a sunny, well-drained position protected from wind. Young leaves are used as a garnish for cooked vegetables. The seeds are used in cabbage, potato and parsnip dishes, and also in some cakes, biscuits and apple pie. Leaves and softer stems can be eaten in salads or cooked with other vegetables.

4 **CARDAMOM**: The cardamom bush is a herbaceous perennial plant of the ginger family and grows nearly 3 m/9 ft high. Cardamom will only grow in a hot climate. It produces slightly pungent, highly aromatic pods holding seeds which are sweet with a camphor-like flavour.

5 **CASSIA**: The bark, unripe seeds and the dried leaves of this plant are all used in cooking. Cassia is regarded as a less expensive substitute for cinnamon and can be used in the same way, although the taste of the bark is not as strong as that of cinnamon. The seeds, also known as Chinese cassia buds, are used in drinks and confectionery and are often added to potpourris.

6 **CAYENNE**: Cayenne pepper, paprika and Tabasco sauce are all made from varieties of capsicum pepper. Cayenne is derived from a hot, red variety of capsicum pepper called 'bird chilli'. Although cayenne is not as hot as some chilli powders it is very pungent and should be used sparingly. Store in an airtight container in small quantities and in a cool, dark place.

7 **CHILLI POWDER**: Made from dried red chillies, this red powder varies in hotness and flavour, from mild to hot.

8 **CINNAMON**: Cinnamon is the bark of a tree which belongs to the laurel family. The cinnamon tree is a tall, thick evergreen tree which prefers tropical climates. The bark is the most important part of the tree – when ground it provides a sweet spice highly valued for both culinary and medicinal usage. The leaves are pointed, smooth and tough and the small creamy-white flowers are followed by dark blue berries. The dried bark is sold in small quills (sticks), usually 7.5-15 cm/3-6 in long, or as powder.

9 **CLOVES**: The clove tree is an evergreen which grows abundantly near tropical sea shores. Cloves are the highly aromatic flower buds of this tree or shrub which is native to the Moluccas or Spice Islands. Nowadays, cloves are mostly grown in Zanzibar and Madagascar.

10 **CORIANDER**: Coriander is a member of the same plant family as parsley. The plant gives off a strong odour which is replaced by a sweet orangey aroma when the seeds are dried. The round, light brown seeds are milder than many other spices and can

be used in large quantities. The taste is fresh with a hint of bitterness and can be improved by gently roasting before grinding.

11 CUMIN: Like coriander and caraway, cumin seed comes from the same plant family as parsley. Cumin is a small and delicate annual which usually grows to 30 cm/1 ft in height. Native to the Middle East, cumin now grows in most hot climates. The small, dark brown, elongated seeds have a rich sweet aroma; their flavour is similarly pungent and they should be used sparingly. Cumin seed is often confused with fennel or anise (both sometimes called 'sweet cumin').

12 FENUGREEK: The fenugreek plant which grows to 30-60 cm/1-2 ft, is a member of the bean and pea family. Its flowers and pods resemble those of the pea. Each long, narrow pod contains ten to twenty, small, hard yellow-brown seeds. The seeds have a

slightly bitter-sweet taste and should be used in moderation. Only when roasted do the seeds give off their pungent aroma. Whole or ground fenugreek is most often used in Indian curries.

13 GINGER: Ginger is an important spice in both the East and the West. Like other tropical plants of the same family, such as turmeric, it is the knobbly root of the ginger plant which is used as a spice. Dried ginger root can be bruised and ground to a powder (its fibres removed) and used as ground ginger, or bruised and infused in the cooking liquid of savoury dishes.

14 MACE: Mace and nutmeg are parts of the fruit of a tropical evergreen tree. Mace blades come from the outer casing of the nutmeg and are bright red when harvested, drying to a deep orange. The flavour of mace is similar to nutmeg.

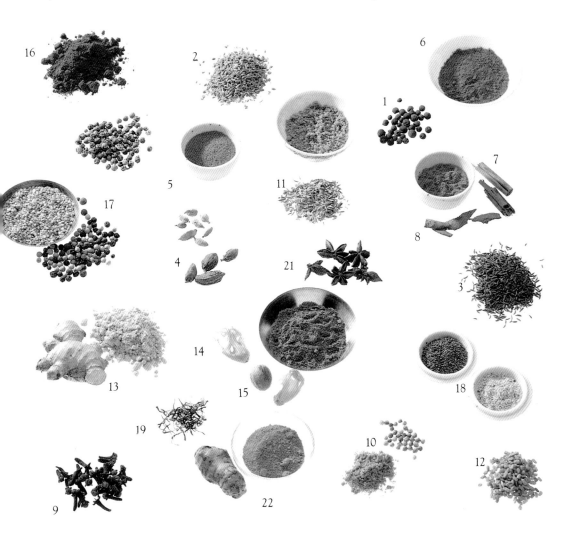

Dry-frying whole spices before grinding mellows the flavour and will add that special touch to your cooking. Spices can be dry-fried individually or in mixtures.

15   NUTMEG: The small, oval shiny nut, about 4 cm/$1^{1}/2$ in long, is dried in its seed coat which is then removed. Nutmeg is slightly milder than mace but has a more nutty flavour – warm and sweetish with a light bitter undertone. Nutmegs can be bought whole or ready-ground. It is best to buy them whole and store in an airtight container. Finely grate as needed.

16   PAPRIKA: Like cayenne pepper, paprika is a finely ground powder made from the fruit of several different chilli plants. The ripe flesh is used for mild, sweet paprika, the seeds are included for more pungent versions. Mild paprika has a light, sweet smell and almost no pungency; the strongest paprika is similar to cayenne pepper.

17   PEPPER: Pepper comes from the tropical trailing vine of the *Piperaceae* family. The vines grow to heights of 3.5 m/$11^{1}/2$ ft and bear long strings of 20-30 small berries which ripen from green to reddish-yellow. Black pepper berries are picked when green and dried whole; for white pepper they are allowed to ripen and turn red and the skin is removed before drying. Green peppercorns are picked when still green and then are usually pickled.

18   POPPY SEEDS: Poppy seeds, sometimes called maw seeds, come from the opium poppy. The plant is related to both the common field poppy and garden varieties. It grows to anything from 30 cm to 1.2 m/1 to 4 ft and bears white, pink or lilac flowers and erect oval seed pods. The tiny, hard seeds are very mild and sweetish and acquire a bitter-sweet nutty flavour when cooked.

19   SAFFRON: Saffron is the most expensive spice in the world. It is the dried stigmas of the flowers of the saffron crocus. The flowers are extracted from the freshly harvested flowers and dried to become irregular, orange-red threads about 4 cm/$1^{1}/2$ in long. It takes about 50,000 stigmas to make up 100 g/$3^{1}/2$ oz of saffron. Saffron imparts a distinctive aroma, bitter honey-like taste and a strong yellow colour to food. It's better to buy the threads and store in an airtight container in a dark place. Ground saffron can vary enormously in quality.

20   SESAME SEEDS: Sesame is a tropical annual with a pungent smell. The plant grows to anything between 60 and 80 cm/2 and $2^{1}/2$ ft. The seed pods contain a large number of small, flat oval seeds in a variety of colours. They may be red, light brown or black and have a rich nutty flavour. Dry roast before use or fry lightly until they just colour and give off a roasted aroma.

21   STAR ANISE: Star anise is the star-shaped fruit of an oriental evergreen of the magnolia family which can reach a height of 7 m/21 ft. When dried it is a brown colour and the flavour is one of pungent aniseed. Whole stars store well in an airtight container and are preferable to the powdered form.

22   TURMERIC: Turmeric is a typical member of the ginger family and, like ginger, it is the knobbly roots or rhizomes which form the cooking spice. The tropical turmeric has spiky yellow flowers and long, shiny pointed leaves, and can grow to a height of 1 m/3 ft. Turmeric has a strong woody aroma and distinctive, pungent flavour. Because of this it should not be used as a cheap substitute for saffron.

23   VANILLA: The dark brown pod of vanilla comes from a type of orchid native to South America. It was discovered by the Spaniards in Mexico. When first picked, the pod is a yellow green and it is only after curing and drying that it becomes the dark brown we associate with vanilla. Essentially a flavouring used in sweet dishes such as ice cream, custards and rice, it is also popular as a flavouring for wine cups, hot chocolate and coffee drinks. The vanilla pod can be used several times and if kept in a jar of sugar will flavour it to make vanilla sugar.

To dry-fry spices, heat a heavy-based frying pan over a medium heat. Add spices and stir constantly until they are evenly browned. Be careful not to let the spices burn. Remove the spices from the pan and allow to cool before grinding.

CHILLIES

The bushy chilli shrub prefers tropical or subtropical climates and grows to between 30 cm and 1.8 m/1 and 6 ft high, depending on the variety. As a general rule, the smaller, narrower and darker the chilli, the greater its pungency. Unripe fresh chillies are usually less pungent than ripe fresh ones, and these in turn are milder than dried chillies.

MUSTARD

Mustard is internationally famous as a condiment and flavouring. The whole seeds are the basis for prepared mustards, and the pungent oil extracted from the seeds and the seeds themselves are also popularly used as culinary spices. There are three main varieties of mustard: black, brown and white. The three plants are similar in appearance and grow to about 1 m/3 ft. All bear tiny, spherical, hard seeds. Brown mustard seeds are most commonly used as an Indian cooking spice.

AT-A-GLANCE SPICE GUIDE

SPICE	SOUPS	MAIN DISHES
Allspice	Beef and minestrone soups	Baked ham, meat loaf, spiced meats
Aniseed	Cream soups	Seafood, pork and poultry dishes
Cardamom	Spiced and curried soups	Curries and spicy dishes of Indian and Middle Eastern origin
Cassia		Chinese dishes and curries
Cayenne pepper	Soups, especially fish and tomato	Curries and spicy dishes, egg dishes
Chilli – fresh	Spicy soups	All curries and spicy meat, poultry, fish and egg dishes
Chilli – powder	Spicy soups	As for fresh chillies
Coriander – seed	Spicy soups	Curries and spicy meat, poultry, fish
Cumin – seed	Spicy soups	Meat, poultry and fish dishes
Curry plant	Fish and spicy soups	Casseroles and curries
Dill – seed	Vegetable soups	Lamb, pork and fish dishes
Fennel – seed		Chicken and fish dishes
Fenugreek		Indian and Middle Eastern dishes
Ginger – fresh		Curries
Ginger – ground		Curries, baked ham and fish dishes
Mace		Fish, chicken, beef and veal dishes
Mustard – powder	Leek and celery soups	Grilled meats, ham, casseroles
Mustard – seed		Curries, pork, rabbit, veal, some fish dishes
Nutmeg	Cream soups	Fish, chicken, egg and cheese dishes, pasta
Paprika	Most soups	Curries, goulashes, pork, beef, veal and fish dishes
Saffron	Especially fish soups	Chicken, fish, turkey and some egg dishes, paella
Turmeric	Curried and spicy soups	Curries, egg and fish dishes
Vanilla		

VEGETABLE DISHES	DESSERTS AND BAKED PRODUCTS	OTHER USES
Carrot, pea and potato salad	Apple desserts such as pies and crumbles, milk puddings	Pickles, confectionery, stewed fruit
Salads, carrots and courgettes (zucchini)	Biscuits, cakes, fresh fruit, especially good with figs	Cheese dips
Vegetable curries	Bread and yeast cakes, custards, fruit salads	Pickles, stewed fruit, savoury and sweet rice dishes
Ground, sprinkle over vegetables		Poached and stewed fruit
		Salad dressings
Spicy vegetable dishes		Salad dressings
Spicy vegetable dishes		Salad dressings, dips, pickles, sauces
Spicy vegetable dishes	Biscuits, cakes, fruit salad	Yogurt dips, salad dressings, stewed fruit
Cabbage, carrots and legume dishes		Pickles, chutneys, marinades, rice dishes
		Stuffings for veal and game
Cucumber, marrow, cabbage and carrots	Biscuits, cakes, fruit salad	Pickles
Potatoes	Biscuits, sprinkle over breads and buns	Salad dressings, sauces for fish
Sprouts used in salads		
	Biscuits, cakes and cooked apples dishes	Marinades
Vegetable curries and spicy legume dishes	Cakes, biscuits, puddings, fruit pies	Pickles, spiced drinks such as mulled wine, stewed fruit
	Biscuits, cakes	Flavour whipped cream, stuffings, pâté
Braised celery and leeks		Salad dressings, stuffings
Cabbage and celery		Stuffings
Cabbage, carrots and root vegetables	Biscuits, cakes, milk puddings, pastries, fruit salads, junket	Stewed fruits, flavour, whipped cream, pâtés
Legume dishes		Rice dishes
	Biscuits, cakes, bread	Savoury rice dishes
	Colouring for cakes and breads	Rice dishes
	Custards, ice cream, milk puddings	Flavour cream, drinks, sugar

INDEX

UK COOKERY EDITOR
Katie Swallow

EDITORIAL
Food Editor: Rachel Blackmore
Editorial Assistant: Ella Martin
Editorial Coordinator: Margaret Kelly
Recipe Development: Sheryle Eastwood, Lucy Kelly, Donna Hay,
Anneka Mitchell, Penelope Peel, Belinda Warn, Loukie Werle
Credits: Recipes page 9 by June Budgen; pages 49, 66 by Pat
Alburey; page 61 by Gordon Grimsdale; pages 64, 65 by Louise
Steel; pages 68, 69 by Annette Grimsdale © Merehurst Limited

COVER
Photography: Ashley Mackevicius
Styling: Wendy Berecry

PHOTOGRAPHY
Per Ericson, Paul Grater, Ray Joyce, Ashley Mackevicius, Harm
Mol, Yanto Noerianto, Andy Payne, Warren Webb

STYLING
Wendy Berecry, Belinda Clayton, Rosemary De Santis, Carolyn
Fienberg, Jacqui Hing, Michelle Gorry

DESIGN AND PRODUCTION
Manager: Sheridan Carter
Layout: Lulu Dougherty
Finished Art: Stephen Joseph
Design: Frank Pithers

Published by J.B. Fairfax Press Pty Ltd
A.C.N. 003 738 430
Formatted by J.B. Fairfax Press Pty Ltd
Output by Adtype, Sydney
Printed by Toppan Printing Co, Hong Kong

Includes Index
1 86343 097 0

Distributed by J.B. Fairfax Press Ltd
9 Trinity Centre, Park Farm Estate
Wellingborough, Northants
Ph: (0933) 402330 Fax: (0933) 402234